A CLOSER LOOK AT COMPARABLE WORTH

A Study of the Basic Questions to be Addressed in Approaching Pay Equity

Robert E. Williams
Lorence L. Kessler

National Foundation for the Study of
Equal Employment Policy
1984

Foreword

"A Closer Look at Comparable Worth" is the first in a series of monographs to be prepared and published by the National Foundation for the Study of Equal Employment Policy. It is a study of the basic questions to be considered in approaching the goal of pay equity for all workers, including particularly women and minorities. Its purpose is to identify the real issues that must be considered and to pose the questions that must be answered in order to determine the wisdom and practicality of the use of comparable worth as a method of achieving pay equity.

The debate over comparable worth has too often confused the undisputed merit of pay equity as a goal with the concept of comparable worth as the method of achieving that goal. This confusion has hampered objective discussion of the very serious practical problems that need to be addressed. These problems include identifying the true causes for the pay gap, only part of which is attributable to employment discrimination, and then developing appropriate remedies. It also is necessary to examine the concept of comparable worth, the assumptions on which it is based, its administrative feasibility, and its relative costs. Underlying all discussions of the concept is its potential for making fundamental changes in the operation of our traditional free market society. While there will be differing views as to the proper answers to these questions, it is essential that they be addressed more analytically and in greater depth than has been done in the past.

The monograph provides an overview of the current debate over the difference in average earnings of male and female workers, a look at the explanations for this pay gap, and a review of the status of existing employment discrimination laws and their applicability to the situation. Also included are a discussion of the role of the market in wage setting, and an explanation of job evaluation that is essential in assessing the comparable worth premise that every job has an intrinsic worth that may be compared with the worth of any other job. The monograph concludes with a review of the potential side effects of comparable worth suggested by various commentators and the relative costs and benefits of the concept as compared to an approach stressing equal opportunity and equal access to better-paying jobs.

The authors of the monograph, Robert E. Williams and Lorence L. Kessler, are attorneys in private practice in Washington, D.C., who specialize in labor management relations and equal employment opportunity law. Throughout the paper, they have focused on raising questions which now must be addressed. They have not purported to supply all of the answers. We hope that the monograph will stimulate the additional thought and study needed to answer those questions, for comparable worth is a concept with broad implications both for our society generally and for each worker individually.

Kenneth C. McGuiness
President
National Foundation for the
Study of Equal Employment Policy

May 1984

About the Foundation

The National Foundation for the Study of Equal Employment Policy is a tax-exempt educational organization formed in 1983 to engage in research on the development of policy and law designed to eliminate all aspects of employment discrimination, whether based on race, color, religion, sex, national origin, age, handicap, veteran status, or other classification. Its purpose is to supply objective explanations of the background, controlling factors, applicable law, and practical considerations involved in dealing with these issues. Included will be analyses of the impact on workers, employers and the general public of existing laws and enforcement policies, government regulations, and private and public sector voluntary programs and assessments of their effectiveness. Both the practical and legal problems involved will be considered and, where necessary, empirical data will be developed.

The issues to be examined will include both those involving the long term development of equal employment policy and questions of more immediate concern arising out of current modifications in equal employment requirements or practices. The latter will meet the public need for timely explanations of the practical effects and possible implications of new developments, such as the issuance of a precedent setting court decision or administrative rule, or the impact of an emerging theory of discrimination.

All research will be conducted by leading experts in the field of equal employment opportunity policy from academic, employer and protected groups. The results will be published in monographs, books and other publications and will be disseminated in such a manner as will best educate and assist the general public. Included will be the development and presentation of seminars and training programs on subjects of critical concern.

The Foundation is an outgrowth of the Equal Employment Advisory Council which comprises a broad segment of the employer community in the United States. The members of the Council are firmly committed to the principles of nondiscrimination and equal employment opportunity. The Foundation will take over the publication and seminar activities formerly performed by the Council. This will include the continuation of the monograph series initiated in 1982 by the Council under which two studies were issued: "Personal Liability of Managers and Supervisors for Corporate EEO Policies and Decisions," and "Employee Selection: Legal and Practical Alternatives to Compliance and Litigation." The Foundation will enlarge the scope of the Council's former activities both from the standpoint of the topics to be covered and their treatment in order to assure that they will be useful to all who seek effective solutions to the problems of employment discrimination.

Table of Contents

The authors wish to acknowledge the valuable assistance provided by the Board of Directors of the National Foundation for the Study of Equal Employment Policy, a group of knowledgeable professionals who are daily engaged in the work of assuring the success of equal employment opportunity programs. Recognition also must be given to the thoughts and efforts contributed by Kenneth C. McGuiness and Douglas S. McDowell to the planning of this study and the preparation of the final manuscript.

Chapter One

FOCUSING ON THE BASIC ISSUES

The average working woman in the United States earns less money than the average working man, and the average minority worker earns less than the average white worker. These earnings differentials, or pay gaps, are at the core of a continuing debate over the concept of "equal pay for jobs of comparable worth."

The term "comparable worth" refers to the theory that jobs of equivalent overall value to the employer or to society ought to be compensated equally, even if the jobs are dissimilar in content. This concept is not to be confused with the principle of "equal pay for equal work," which requires equal compensation for jobs that require substantially the same skills, effort and responsibility and are performed under similar working conditions. The "equal pay for equal work" principle is part of existing federal and state law. Thus, under the law today, a female maintenance worker is entitled to be paid the same as a male maintenance worker doing the same job. Under the concept of comparable worth, a female clerical employee could demand to be paid the same as a male maintenance worker on the theory that the two jobs were of similar value to the employer or to society.

Interest in the comparable worth issue has tended to focus on the existence of the male/female pay gap and the demand that it be eliminated, rather than on the causes of the gap and the best methods for dealing with those causes. It is essential that these basic issues be given greater attention by identifying and examining the causes of the pay gap and the extent to which the gap is or is not the result of discrimination by employers. Then,

1

the analysis can focus on the adequacy of existing laws to remedy such discrimination and the merits of comparable worth as a practical solution.

The debate over comparable worth is often characterized as a debate over "pay equity." In fact, however, there is no argument about the desirability of fair and equitable compensation practices. With rare exceptions business men and women understand that, regardless of moral and equitable considerations, it simply does not make good business sense to tolerate inequities in pay for any segment of the workforce. To do so invites bad employee relations. Workers who feel they are discriminatorily underpaid are likely either to leave, taking needed skills and experience with them, or to stay in their jobs but lose the incentive to be productive. Most employers, therefore, continually seek to maintain pay rates that will be perceived as equitable by all groups in their employ. Consequently, pay equity is not really a proposition to be debated; it is a goal widely shared by employers and employees alike. The real issue is how pay equity can best be determined, achieved and maintained.

Too often discussions of the pay gap begin with the assumption that most, if not all, of the differential is the result of discrimination by employers. Serious doubt as to the accuracy of this premise has been raised by a number of well-documented studies. At this point in the debate, it seems self-evident that simple assumptions cannot be the basis for effective solutions. Careful identification of the specific problems to be solved is required.

In examining these problems and potential solutions, a number of responsible experts have raised questions about the effectiveness and practicality of any system of legally mandated comparable worth as a means of achieving pay equity. Basic questions are: Does a job have an intrinsic worth to society or to the employer, separate and apart from the price that can be obtained for it in the labor market? If so, how can such worth be measured and used in comparisons of the worth of different jobs? If such comparisons are to be made, who will make them: employers, courts, or administrative agencies? What would be the standards for making such comparisons and who will decide what those standards are? What are the potential economic and social consequences of requiring pay rates to be based on a theory

2

of comparable worth? Are there alternative approaches that are or potentially would be more effective in narrowing the pay gap?

Recognition that a pay gap exists is only a starting point for exploration of these more difficult issues. This monograph will focus on the meaning of the pay gap statistics, the arguments advanced by advocates of the comparable worth concept, and the numerous practical and policy questions that arise in response to that concept. It is hoped that focusing the debate in these directions will contribute to a better understanding of the real issues surrounding it, and thus to a more favorable climate in which to work toward the common goal of pay equity for all American workers.

Chapter Two

AN OVERVIEW OF THE DEBATE

When the earnings of American workers are broken down according to the sex, race, and other characteristics of the individual employee, it is apparent that:

(1) the earnings of the average male employee exceed the earnings of the average female employee;

(2) the earnings of the average white employee exceed those of the average black employee; and

(3) the earnings of the average black employee exceed those of the average Hispanic employee.

The amount, causes, and implications of these differences are all debatable, but there is no disputing that such differentials— or pay gaps—do exist.

Until very recently, a 59-cent figure was frequently cited in discussions about the extent of the male/female pay gap. It was typically said that the average working woman received only 59 cents for every dollar in pay received by the average working man. That figure was based on gross annual statistical comparisons made by the U.S. Census Bureau which showed that the ratio of the average earnings of full-time working women to those of full-time working men throughout the 1970's ran at approximately 59 percent. These figures are not static, however, and the most recent available statistics indicate a somewhat higher ratio of women's earnings to men's. Thus, for the final quarter of 1983, the statistics show that the average male worker earned $393 per week and the average female worker earned $260 per week, or approximately 66.2% as much as the average male.

Other specific ratios for the final quarter of 1983 show that the average black male's earnings were 78.1 percent of the average white male's, and the average Hispanic male's earnings were 68.1 percent of the average white male worker's. During the same period, the average white female worker earned 67.1 percent as much as the average of all male workers. Black female workers earned 60.8 percent of male earnings and Hispanic females 56.4 percent.[1]

Women's Earnings

It is the first statistic mentioned above, the overall ratio between average male and female earnings, that has received the most attention. A significant fact underlying this statistical gap is that men and women are not evenly distributed among the different jobs in our society. This factor itself is also part of the ongoing debate. Most women workers continue to be concentrated in relatively few occupations. Approximately 80 percent of all women workers are employed in just 25 of the 420 occupational categories listed by the Department of Labor. Thus, more than 95 percent of all secretaries and more than 95 percent of all registered nurses are females. More than 80 percent of all elementary school teachers and more than 80 percent of all librarians are females. The average wage in predominantly-female occupations tends to be lower than the average wage in predominantly-male occupations.

---

[1]The percentages in the text refer to data in the report on "Earnings of Workers and Their Families: Fourth Quarter 1983," released by the Department of Labor, Bureau of Labor Statistics, on January 30, 1984. The median usual *weekly* earnings for full-time wage and salary workers are as follows:

	Male	Female	Female as % of Male
White	402	264	65%
Black	314	239	76%
Hispanic	277	222	80%

The 59-cent figure often cited in the past was a calculation based on a comparison of *annual* earnings of women and men who worked year-round and who were primarily full-time workers. It has been observed that the "annual" statistic is primarily of interest because of its availability for many years but that the more recently available "weekly" statistic is a more accurate representation of the size of the male/female pay gap. See J. O'Neill, "The Trend in the Sex Differential in Wages" (1983), p. 4.

6

A statistical gap also appears when the gross average earnings of women employed in some of the higher-paying predominantly-male occupations are compared with those of the average man in such occupations. The Bureau of Labor Statistics reports that in eight specific occupations—lawyers, computer science analysts, health administrators, engineers, physicians and dentists, elementary and secondary school administrators, personnel and labor relations workers, and operations and systems analysts—the average woman's earnings as a percent of the average man's earnings ranged from 64 percent (in personnel and labor relations) to 82 percent (among operations and systems analysts). It must be noted that these are gross statistics, and they are not adjusted to reflect the many factors that may influence the female-male pay ratio within specific occupations. As the Commissioner of the Bureau of Labor Statistics has pointed out, "Seniority, level of responsibililty, quality of performance, and geographic location are only a few of such factors."[2]

In addition to being concentrated into relatively few occupational categories, the majority of working women are employed in the country's lowest paying industries. A ranking of industries prepared by the Bureau of Labor Statistics in 1982 showed that those industries with higher percentages of female employees often tended to have lower average hourly earnings. For example, the apparel and textile products industry had the highest percentage of women employees among the 52 industries ranked, but it was 50th in average hourly earnings. The apparel and accessory stores industry ranked fourth in the proportion of women workers, but was last in average hourly earnings. Conversely, the bituminous coal and lignite mining industry ranked 52nd in percentage of women employees but had the highest average hourly earnings. The primary metal industries ranked 47th in the proportion of women workers, but were 6th in average hourly earnings.[3]

---

[2]See testimony of Janet Norwood, Commissioner of Bureau of Labor Statistics, Joint Hearings on Pay Equity before the Subcommittees on Human Resources, Civil Service, and Compensation and Employee Benefits of the Committee on Post Office and Civil Service, House of Representatives, 97th Cong., 2d Sess. September 16, 1982, p. 55.
[3]See table accompanying testimony of Commissioner Norwood, *ibid*, pp. 58-62.

The Comparable Worth Approach

These statistics provide the backdrop for the current debate. On one side of the issue, it is argued that the pay gap between males and females and the concentration of women in relatively low-paying jobs are evidence that our equal employment opportunity laws have not worked. It is suggested that our society historically has undervalued particular jobs done by women simply because that work has been performed by women. Thus, it is argued, new laws are needed (or interpretations of existing laws should be expanded) to assure that women in traditionally-female jobs are compensated fairly. The most common remedy suggested by those arguing for broader employment laws has been that employers should be required to provide equal pay for jobs which, although different, are of comparable worth to the employer or to society generally.

The comparable worth approach is fundamentally different from the "equal pay for equal work" requirement embodied in existing laws. "Equal pay for equal work" means that where a man and a woman perform equal work, requiring substantially the same skill, effort and responsibility in the same establishment, they must receive equal pay. Those who endorse the comparable worth approach argue that "equal pay for equal work" cannot by itself raise the wages in those predominantly-female jobs which employ the great majority of women workers.

On the opposite side of the debate are many who support fair and equitable pay practices, including equal pay for equal work, but who question the comparable worth theory. Among these voices are employers, labor economists, government officials and others who are committed to eliminating sex bias in employment practices. They neither dispute the existence of a male/female pay gap nor quarrel with the goal of closing that gap. But they do question whether the comparable worth theory is a practical approach and maintain that existing laws can effectively eliminate any portion of the pay gap that is attributable to employment discrimination.

Differences in Worker Characteristics

In the following chapters, the questions raised by the comparable worth theory will be examined in detail. The discussion begins with a closer look at the difference in earnings between men and women and the various factors that have combined to create the pay gap. In an objective analysis of comparable worth, it is important to distinguish between barriers to pay parity imposed by employers, on the one hand, and the effects of societal attitudes, customs, and restrictions on individuals before and after they enter the labor market on the other.

Thus, in Chapter Three, some of the differences which distinguish the average working man and woman are examined.[4] For example, studies show that the average working man remains in the labor force continuously after leaving school, but the average working woman does not. Also, the studies reveal that even those women who ultimately do spend many years in the work force often did not plan to do so initially. As a result, women as a group have tended not to invest as much time in preparing for careers with high long-term earnings potential as have their male counterparts. In addition, the large numbers of relatively inexperienced women who have entered the work force in recent years have drawn down the overall average of women's earnings.

Studies also show that the earnings gap is definitely narrowed when allowances are made for differences between men and women in education, work experience, seniority, number of hours worked, and continuity within the work force. Because not all of these factors are readily quantifiable, however, their total impact on the pay gap is still a subject of considerable controversy. Also, while the remainder of the gap is closely linked to the concentration of women within certain traditional occupations, again, it is difficult to measure exactly how much of that concentration arises out of individual preferences and traditional cultural patterns, rather than exclusionary hiring and promotion practices by employers. Consequently, both the true size and the causes of the pay gap remain open to serious questions.

---

[4]The goal of our society's equal employment policy is to assure equal opportunity to *individuals*, regardless of their sex or race. Any discussion of the pay gap, however, necessarily involves looking at men and women as groups, even though many individuals in each group differ from the "average" working man or the "average" working woman.

9

The Effect of Existing Laws

Although it is now generally accepted that a number of nondiscriminatory factors do contribute to the pay gap, a portion remains that cannot be explained by statistical analyses. This naturally gives rise to the contention that at least some part of this unexplained residual is the result of discriminatory practices by employers, such as relegating women to low-paying jobs, paying women less than men who do the same work, or deliberately setting pay rates lower in certain jobs because they are held mostly by women. But such practices are already prohibited by law. Accordingly, those who question the comparable worth doctrine argue that there is no evidence that any portion of the gap caused by employer discrimination in fact is beyond the reach of effective enforcement of existing equal employment opportunity laws.

Comparable worth advocates often complain that existing laws and policies are inadequate to provide a timely solution, pointing out that the pay gap still remains twenty years after the major federal laws prohibiting sex and race discrimination in employment were first enacted. Others counter that in the past two decades there has been substantial progress which does not show up in the gross statistics usually cited in discussions of the pay gap. Employers also point out that the societal patterns that underlie much of the pay gap have changed gradually over the past two decades, with much of the change occurring in the last ten years, at least in part as a result of employers' voluntary affirmative action programs and their commitment to the goals of equal opportunity. The effects of these programs, they say, have only begun to be reflected in the overall statistics. Pointing to the changing character of both U.S. industry and life styles, they predict that policies assuring full job mobility to women and minority workers will lead to a substantial narrowing of the pay gap during the coming decade.

The existing federal laws involved in this debate and the specific practices they prohibit are examined in Chapter Four. That chapter also discusses how courts have interpreted existing laws to prohibit sex and race bias in compensation practices while generally avoiding making judgments about evaluations of the worth of different jobs. Also raised in Chapter Four are various basic questions which the courts have not yet answered fully, such as how allegations of wage discrimination are to be proved, and how defenses of legitimate, nondiscriminatory compensation practices are to be structured. In the context of this legal uncertainty, concern is expressed that court decisions such as the multi-million dollar award by the trial court in *AFSCME v. State of Washington*,[5] which gave legally-binding effect to the state's own job value determinations, could have the unfortunate result of discouraging other employers from undertaking job evaluation studies to try to improve their compensation practices.

The Market Factor

The central issues in the debate over comparable worth— the worth of a particular job and how it is to be determined— are discussed in Chapter Five in the context of the influence of market factors on compensation. Included are a review of the basic market factors affecting wage determinations and of differing schools of thought about how the labor market operates. This discussion also examines the significance of market factors in determining whether differences in pay rates have been caused by discrimination. It is noted that a system that fails to recognize legitimate market-based differences in pay rates for different jobs would require the establishment of new mechanisms for evaluating job worth as a basic part of our equal employment opportunity enforcement system. But what those mechanisms would be, and how they would work, have not yet been defined anywhere in the current debate.

Job Evaluation

Advocates of comparable worth have tended to dismiss objections about the complexity of comparing the worth of different jobs on the ground that employers routinely compare dissimilar jobs for the purpose of setting salaries. Representative Patricia Schroeder, who chaired one of several Congressional subcommittees which held hearings on pay equity, has expressed similar

---

[5]See 578 F. Supp. 846, 33 Fair Empl. Prac. Cas. (BNA) 808, 33 Empl. Prac. Dec. (CCH) 33,976 (W.D. Wash. 1983).

skepticism toward arguments about the difficulty of comparing different jobs:

> The point is that every employer is daily in the business of comparing the value of differing jobs. Being designed for employers who want to hold down their wage bills, these systems tend to reflect market discrimination against women. What is needed is a bias-free job classification system which can determine the comparable worth of jobs. Such a system would tell us how much more a teacher is worth to society than a parking lot attendant, of how much more value a nurse is than a gardener. Once we learn how undervalued female jobs are we can develop a reasonable strategy to implement true pay equity.[6]

But can job evaluation techniques be made sufficiently objective to eliminate any potentially biased or otherwise controversial value judgments from the process? Many experts argue that these issues cannot be dealt with so simply. Moreover, implicit in the statement of Rep. Schroeder and others like it is the assumption that jobs should be compensated in proportion to their value to *society*. But in a free-market economic system, it has traditionally been the value of the job to the purchaser of the services performed—that is, its value to the *employer*—that has governed rates of pay.

The concepts and practice of job evaluation are examined in Chapter Six. There it is noted that, while many employers do use job evaluation systems to place their own values on jobs, and while companies and unions sometimes agree upon sets of standards that will be used in evaluating jobs and fixing pay rates, experts nevertheless question whether a court, a legislature, or a regulatory agency can use job evaluation techniques to impose and enforce pay equity. Rather, they suggest that job evaluation is at best a systematic way of making subjective value judgments, useful as a managerial and administrative tool but not suitable as a means of implementing a legal standard requiring comparable worth. Also, even the staunchest advocates of job evaluation admit that it is useful only in a context that recognizes and takes account of labor market considerations and the economic position of the employing firm. Thus, another serious,

---

[6]Joint Hearings on Pay Equity before the Subcommittees on Human Resources, Civil Service, Compensation and Employee Benefits of the House of Representatives Committee on Post Office and Civil Service, 97th Cong. 2d Sess., September 16, 1982, pp. 12-13.

unanswered question central to the comparable worth debate is whether job evaluations can produce valuations sufficiently dependable and objective to serve as a workable legal standard.

Unintended Consequences

In its study on *Women, Work, and Wages,* the National Academy of Sciences observed that, because comparable worth involves intervention in the operation of market forces, it has the potential of creating unintended, counterproductive consequences.[7] A number of experts who have examined the issue have concluded that such consequences would in fact accompany implementation of comparable worth. In Chapter Seven, the observations of these experts are reviewed. Their analyses cast doubt on the wisdom of adopting comparable worth as a mandatory employment policy without first finding satisfactory answers to the many practical questions that have been raised about its operation. Of particular concern is the general agreement among these experts that comparable worth could lead to significant unemployment or dislocation of many workers in the very group it is intended to benefit, that is, the women in relatively low-paying, predominantly-female jobs.

It has sometimes been argued that a comparable worth policy could be implemented without disruptive consequences in the United States, because the government of Australia assertedly implemented such a policy a few years ago. Economists who have analyzed the Australian experience, however, now challenge this assertion and point out adverse effects in that country as well as basic differences between the Australian and U.S. wage-setting systems. These issues are examined as part of Chapter Seven.

---

[7]National Academy of Sciences Committee on Occupational Classification and Analysis, *Women, Work, and Wages: Equal Pay for Jobs of Equal Value,* eds., D. Treiman and H. Hartmann (1981) pp. 67, 92. The NAS Committee concluded that job evaluation plans provide measures of job worth that, under certain circumstances, might be used to discover and reduce wage discrimination for persons covered by a given plan. They suggested that job evaluation needs further study and development, but then warned that

> we have not been able to make any assessment of what the social and economic consequences may be of implementing wage policies based on the principle of equal pay for jobs of equal worth. This is an extremely complex question, with no clear answers. . . . We do, however, want to call attention to the need to give careful thought to the possible impact of implementation of a policy of equal pay for jobs of equal worth on the economic viability of firms as well as on employment opportunities for women and minorities.

Costs of Comparable Worth and Alternative Approaches

A final question that is raised frequently as a part of this debate is how much a policy of comparable worth would cost. Advocates of such a policy emphasize that discriminatory pay practices cannot be justified on the ground that they save employers money. Others generally agree that cost considerations should not be a primary factor in judging the merits of comparable worth. But, they caution that it would be imprudent to implement such a policy without having at least some estimate of what it would cost, not only in increased wages but also in potential administrative expenses. Several cost estimates are discussed in Chapter Eight. As part of a cost-benefit analysis of comparable worth, consideration also is given to whether there may be a workable alternative. Would a strong policy to assure women equal access to higher-paying jobs, combined with effective enforcement of existing equal pay laws, have the potential for narrowing the wage gap without the negative consequences attached to the comparable worth theory?

Some of the most responsible voices in the pay equity debate have acknowledged that there are fundamental aspects of the comparable worth theory that need additional study. For example, Eleanor Holmes Norton, former chair of the Equal Employment Opportunity Commission, has said:

> Employers have often indicated concern that remedies for pay discrimination would necessitate precipitous and prohibitively large wage increases that would have dislocating effects. They believe that absent intolerable bureaucratic intrusions, there is no alternative to the use of prevailing market mechanisms to set wages.

> Of course, these mechanisms have been altered already by collective bargaining and by governmental mechanisms that range from minimum wage provisions to adjustments mandated by the Equal Pay Act even where pay discrimination has resulted from supply and demand market conditions. Still, the questions raised by remedies for comparable pay discrimination present new questions that require attention.[8]

The issues discussed in the following chapters clearly underscore this recognition that serious questions surrounding comparable worth remain unanswered.

---

[8]Testimony of Eleanor Holmes Norton, Joint Hearings on Pay Equity before the Subcommittees on Human Resources, Civil Service, Compensation and Employee Benefits of the House of Representatives Committee on Post Office and Civil Service, 97th Cong. 2d Sess., September 16, 1982, pp. 43.

Chapter Three

LOOKING BEHIND THE
PAY GAP STATISTICS

As indicated in the preceding chapters, serious questions have been raised about the underlying causes of the male/female pay gap and the extent to which it is valid to assume that the gap is a product of discrimination. To answer these questions, it is necessary first to explore the reasons for the differences in male and female earnings in more detail.

Variation In The Pay Gap

There is not simply one "pay gap." Within our society, wage differentials among workers exist "by occupation, by industry, by race, and by sex, to list only a few. Since groups of workers who differ in one of these dimensions are unlikely to be the same in all others, particular differentials are seldom observed in pure form."[1] The earnings differential between male and female workers varies, for example, with the race of the workers being observed. As the statistics in the preceding chapter indicate, at the end of 1983, white female workers' earnings were 67.1 percent of those of the average male, while black females earned 60.8 percent and Hispanic female workers 56.4 percent of the average male worker.[2] The differential also varies with the age of the workers being compared and their

---

[1]A. Rees, *The Economics of Work and Pay* (2d ed. 1979), p. 153. Professor Rees notes that in order to accurately measure the differences in pay between groups that result solely from one classification, such as sex, it is necessary to standardize for worker differences in their other characteristics, such as occupation and industry. *Ibid.*

[2]"Earnings of Workers and Their Families: Fourth Quarter 1983," released by the Department of Labor, Bureau of Labor Statistics, January 30, 1984.

occupations. For example, for employees between 20 and 24 years of age, women's earnings are 77.7 percent of the earnings of men; for workers between 25 and 34 years old, the ratio is 68.8 percent; and for those between 35 and 44 years old, the ratio is 56.2 percent.[3] Examining various occupations, we find that for craft workers, women's earnings are 61.3 percent of men's earnings. For health workers (other than physicians, dentists and related practitioners), women's earnings are 90.5 percent of the earnings of men. Among college and university teachers, they are 74.6 percent of male earnings, while among elementary and secondary school teachers the ratio is 78.1 percent. For accountants, the ratio is 64.4 percent.[4]

In addition to occupation, the number of hours worked is another factor which causes the differential to fluctuate. The gross statistics cited at the beginning of Chapter Two showed the average wages of a full-time female employee to be 66.2 percent of the average wages of a full-time male employee. To be included in this pool of data as a full-time worker, it is necessary only that the individual work at least 35 hours per week. Within this group, however, full-time women workers average fewer hours per week than full-time men workers; more full-time men than women work in excess of 41 hours a week. If this factor is taken into account, the differential narrows. According to economist Dr. June O'Neill of the Urban Institute:

> [Women's earnings expressed as a percentage of men's earnings are] several percentage points higher . . . within narrower ranges of hours worked per week: 74 percent for those working 35 hours, 68 percent for those working 40 hours and 73 percent for those working 41 or more hours a week. The weighted average female-male earnings ratio using either the women's or the men's distribution of full-time hours worked is approximately 69 percent.[5]

---

[3]J. O'Neill, "The Trend in the Sex Differential in Wages," a paper presented at Conference on Trends in Women's Work, Education and Family Building, White House Conference Center, Chelwood Gate, Sussex, England, May 31 to June 3, 1983. These ratios are based on 1980 statistics. Dr. O'Neill is Director of the Urban Institute's Program of Policy Research on Women and Families.
[4]See "The Earnings Gap Between Women and Men" published by the Women's Bureau of the U.S. Department of Labor (1979). These statistics represent data for the year 1977 from the Current Population Reports of the Census Bureau.
[5]J. O'Neill, "The Trend in the Sex Differential in Wages," p. 6. See also the discussion of earnings differences in S. Levitan, et al., *Human Resources and Labor Markets* (1981), pp. 282-285.

Distribution of Workers In Different Industries

An additional factor to be considered when examining the pay gap is that women workers are not distributed among various industries to the same degree as men. Indeed, as demonstrated by the Bureau of Labor Statistics data discussed in Chapter Two, the majority of working women are employed in the nation's lowest paying industries. One study of the industrial distribution of workers on the basis of race and sex found that the more extreme differences in distribution were by sex. Among white males the highest proportion of workers was employed in construction (10.2 percent), with retail trade (8.9 percent), machinery manufacturing (7.8 percent), government (6.1 percent) and educational services (5.9 percent) ranking next. The distribution of black males was also fairly diversified, with the highest percentages being in government employment (9.3 percent), construction (8.2 percent), transportation (8.2 percent), motor vehicle manufacturing (7.4 percent), and educational services (7.3 percent). Employment patterns among female workers were found to be quite different from those for males. More than 50 percent of white female heads of households in the study were employed in just three industries: retail trade, medical and dental services, and educational services. Black female workers were similarly concentrated. More than 50 percent of the black female heads of households were employed in three industries: medical and dental services, educational services, and personal services.[6]

Nondiscriminatory Factors Affecting The Pay Gap

These preliminary observations suggest that a variety of factors contribute to the earnings differential that appears when two groups of employees are compared. Not all of these factors can be measured and accounted for with absolute precision, but most observers agree that there are identifiable reasons, unrelated to any employment discrimination, that explain a substantial portion of the earnings differential between men and women.

---

[6]T. Parcel and C. Mueller, "*Ascription and Labor Markets*, (1983), pp. 126-131. *See also* testimony and charts presented by the Commissioner of Bureau of Labor Statistics, Joint Hearings on Pay Equity before the Subcommittees on Human Resources, Civil Service, and Compensation and Employee Benefits of the Committee on Post Office and Civil Service, House of Representatives, 97th Cong., 2d Sess., Sept. 16, 1982, pp. 51-62.

These reasons include a number of factors that are significant in any earnings comparison, not just comparisons between male and female averages. For example, in numerous studies comparing the earnings of certain white males to those of other white males, it is apparent that more experienced workers normally receive higher pay than comparable workers who have spent less time in the labor force.[7] This same factor of work experience has an observable impact in creating the difference between average male and average female earnings. Studies show that women as a group have tended to enter and leave the labor force more frequently than men for various reasons, including reasons associated with the bearing and raising of children. This results not only in women as a group having less overall work force experience, but also in their having less continuous work experience than men. When women do leave and reenter the workforce intermittently, "they may have lost valuable time in their chosen fields."[8] Several studies have found that women in the workforce, on average, have less work experience, seniority and up-to-date skills than men, at least in part because of these interruptions. The studies also point out that both the length of time spent in an occupation and the worker's tenure in a particular job have a noticeable effect on wages. Similarly, Census Bureau studies of lifetime earnings show that the continuity of lifetime work experience is a very important determinant of annual earnings levels.[9] Additional studies which allow for earnings com-

---

[7]See J.L. Medoff and K.G. Abraham, "Are Those Paid More Really More Productive? The Case of Experience," *Journal of Human Resources*, XVI, 2 (1981). See also, J.L. Medoff and K.G. Abraham, "Experience, Performance, and Earnings," *The Quarterly Journal of Economics*, December 1980 ("There is abundant evidence that earnings grow with labor market experience over most of a normal worklife.").

[8]S. Bianchi and D. Spain, *American Women: Three Decades of Change*, Bureau of the Census, Special Demographic Analyses, (1983), p. 24. It may be observed that the statistical distortion that arises from this fact—that is, that the participation of the average woman in the workforce has been more intermittent than that of the average man—would appear to be largely eliminated when the earnings of never-married working women are compared to the earnings of never-married working men. Among various groups of women workers, the never-married women "are most likely to have had continuous work histories and so their earnings suffered least." D. Bellante and M. Jackson, *Labor Economics: Choice in Labor Markets* (1979), p. 198. Statistics for never-married white workers showed female earnings to be 86 percent of male earnings. *Ibid*. A more recent comparison of all never-married workers showed the average woman earning 84 percent as much as the average man. See U.S. Bureau of Labor Statistics, Handbook of Labor Statistics, table 60 (1979).

[9]"Lifetime Earnings Estimates for Men and Women in the United States: 1979," Current Population Reports, Series P-60, No. 139, U.S. Department of Commerce, Bureau of the Census (1983).

parisons among women with no break in employment, women with a break in employment of one year, and women with breaks in employment of longer duration demonstrate the significant impact such breaks can have on total earnings potential.[10]

Changes in societal patterns and employment policies that may eventually lessen the impact of this factor on the size of the pay gap are just beginning to be observed. For example, liberalized maternity leave policies currently offered by many employers, coupled with a greater willingness on the part of some husbands today to share in child-rearing that traditionally has been the responsibility of women, now make it possible for more women with children to avoid serious disruption of their careers. The increased availability of day care facilities, with employer sponsorship in some instances, also supports this trend.[11] Still, such developments have only recently begun to spread, and the overall pay gap statistics cited today continue to be affected significantly by the historic pattern of women's relative lack of continuity in the workforce.

A related phenomenon is reflected in the Department of Labor's finding that, on an average, men have tended to expect a more extended working career and have shown more willingness to invest in greater future earnings potential by way of job training, job searches, education and other long range income-increasing techniques. The Department's study found:

> . . . empirical support . . . for the hypothesis that expected future labor force attachment will be an important determinant of accumulation of general human capital through investment in on-the-job training. It has been suggested elsewhere that young women tend to underestimate the likelihood of their being in the labor force after completing childraising. Our results are consistent with the hypothesis that young women who do not desire future labor force attachment will not acquire much general training in job skills in the initial stages of their working lives. Consequently, it seems likely that

---

[10]J. Stevens and R. Herriot, "Current Earnings Differentials of Men and Women: Some Exploratory Regression Analysis," *ASA Proceedings of the Social Statistics Section, 1975*, pp. 673-678.

[11]In "Employers and Child Care: Establishing Services Through the Workplace," published by the Women's Bureau of the U.S. Department of Labor (1982), the Director of the Women's Bureau observed that many private sector employers have recognized that finding or providing child care services for employees can be very beneficial. "At many companies, personnel policies are being reshaped to permit a realistic blending of job and family duties, creating a new harmony that keeps parent-employees on the job with reduced stress and higher morale."

many young women will be at a serious disadvantage if they attempt to reenter the labor force after raising a family.[12]

Again, there are positive indications that these patterns have begun to change and that many women preparing for and entering the labor force today have a different set of expectations than even their recent predecessors.[13] But as long as the overall class of women in the workforce includes a substantial number of individuals who have not prepared for work with the expectation of a long-term career, the average woman's earnings are likely to continue to lag behind those of the average man.

Even as traditional patterns change, it must be recognized that societal traditions continue to influence choices made by individual women, and thereby contribute to the size of the pay gap. Regardless of one's views of these traditions, they are factors that must be considered separate from discrimination by employers. For example, women as a group, to a greater extent than men, have traditionally assumed the primary role for child-raising responsibilities.[14] If, as a result of these responsibilities, individual women have taken certain kinds of jobs more often than individual men because the hours and other job requirements have been seen as compatible with child-raising responsibilities, should the presence of these women in predominantly-female occupations be regarded as a result of employment discrimination? Or, if women, to a greater extent than men, acting on individual preferences or on advice from parents or guidance counselors, have tended to prepare themselves for jobs with limited long-range advancement potential in the belief that they would be in the workforce for only a limited time, are they to be regarded as victims of job segregation? And if the large

---

[12]*Years for Decision: A Longitudinal Study of the Educational and Labor Market Experience of Young Women*, Vol. 4, p. 161 (footnote omitted). See also O'Neill, "The Trend in the Sex Differential in Wages," pp. 17-19.

[13]Recent studies show significant increases in female enrollment in college and graduate school programs. In 1979, for the first time since World War II, women college students outnumbered men students. Between 1972 and 1980, there was a 22% increase in the proportion of master's degrees awarded to women, and the number of doctoral degrees given to women increased by 83%. Similarly, between 1972 and 1981, the number of women enrolled in law schools rose from 9,075 to 39,728, an increase of 337%. See "Title IX: The Half Full, Half Empty Glass," National Advisory Council on Women's Educational Programs (Fall 1981), pp. 29-31.

[14]See, for example, discussion of married women in the workforce in S. Levitan, G. Mangum, and R. Marshall, *Human Resources and Labor Markets* (1981), pp. 282-285. See also the responses to a 1982 Market Opinion Research national survey reported by Barbara Everitt Bryant in "Women, and the 59-Cent Dollar," *American Demographics*, Vol. 5, No. 8 (August 1983), pp. 28-31.

numbers of women in a few occupations that seem to be most compatible with such patterns and expectations results in an oversupply that drives down the market price of labor in those occupations, is this a problem to be remedied by employment discrimination law? Today's workforce reflects a social structure in which women's roles have traditionally been different from men's, but now are rapidly changing.[15]

A factor closely related to these societal trends that also has had an important effect on the size of the pay gap in recent years has been the tremendous influx into the labor market of women without prior job experience. Between 1947 and 1980, the number of women in the labor force increased by 173 percent (from 16.7 million to 45.6 million) while the number of men in the labor force increased by only 43 percent (from 44.2 million to 63.4 million).[16]. The greatest increase in female participation rates in the 1960's and 1970's was among women aged 20-44. The largest increase during the 1960's was for 20-24 year olds followed by the 25-34 year old women. In the 1970's "substantial increases were registered for all women under 45, and the increase in the rate for 25-34 year old women was more than twice the overall increase."[17] In 1979, the women aged 20-24 years old had a labor force participation rate of 69.3 percent exceeding that of every other age group.[18] The significance of these recent

---

[15]See the discussion on the significance of individual worker preference in the explanation of the labor market in Chapter Five.

[16]S. Bianchi and D. Spain, *American Women: Three Decades of Change*, Bureau of the Census, (1983), p. 15. Studies by the Bureau of Labor Statistics indicate that the "number of married women (husband present) in the labor force rose by nearly 6 million over the 1970s"—representing an increase of approximately 28 percent, the largest increase for this group "in any decade in U.S. history." B. Johnson and E. Waldman, *Monthly Labor Review*, Oct. 1981, p. 36. Between 1970 and 1983, the number of divorced, separated, widowed or never-married women who were in the labor force supporting families doubled, an increase of 2.9 million workers. B. Johnson and E. Waldman, *Monthly Labor Review*, Dec. 1983, p. 30.

[17]Bianchi and Spain, *ibid*, p. 17. Professor Eli Ginzberg, who directed the studies of women's lifestyles conducted by the Conservation of Human Resources Project at Columbia University has suggested that the significantly increasing number of women entering the workforce is "the single most outstanding phenomenon of our century." In comparing the labor force participation rate for women in the U.S. with that of women in Europe, Commissioner Janet Norwood of the Bureau of Labor Statistics has pointed out that, other than in Scandanavia, the extent of economic activity by women in Europe remains well behind the U.S. level. J. Norwood, "Labor Market Contrasts: United States and Europe," *Monthly Labor Review*, U.S. Department of Labor, August 1983, p. 4.

[18]See discussions of patterns and ages of women workers in S. Levitan, et al., *Human Resources and Labor Markets* (1981), p. 282, and in J. O'Neill, "The Trend in the Sex Differential in Wages" (1983).

increases in the workforce participation rate of relatively younger and less experienced women has been noted by the Bureau of Census:

> In part, the lack of improvement [in the male-female wage differential] since the 1950s reflects the increase in labor force participation of women from 35 percent to 50 percent in that time span. The entry of large numbers of inexperienced women into the work force undoubtedly drove down the average wages of women. Thus, there may be some improvement in relative wage rates of experienced female workers hidden in the averages for all women workers.[19]

In other words, the Census Bureau study indicates that there may have been progress in improving the relative earnings position of women in recent years that does not show up in gross comparisons of average male and female workers' earnings. Gains already achieved through expanded job mobility and other non-discrimination policies may be masked in the gross averages by the disproportionate number of women now in the labor force at or near the entry pay levels.

In short, there are numerous factors reflected in the male/female earnings differential that are not the result of sex discrimination by employers. Not all of these readily identifiable factors are readily quantified.[20] Those generally accepted factors that can be measured and quantified, however, can be worked into the calculations for measuring the differential. As the Bureau of Labor Statistics and numerous labor economists have pointed out, the earnings gap is narrowed as more of these economic and

---

[19]Davis and Spiegelman, *The Comparable Worth Controversy*, SRI International Research Report 660 (1982), p. 1.

[20]Professor George Milkovich has observed that while actual pay decisions are decentralized at the level of an employer, an employee, and perhaps a union, most analysis of the earnings gap is conducted at aggregate levels:

> Unfortunately, studies based on these aggregate models often do not adequately include factors used in wage setting practices, such as differences in employee work behaviors; in the education, skills, and abilities to perform specific jobs; in the specific content of the work; in the interaction or match between employee qualifications and the work requirements; in the employer's wage policies; or in union objectives and relationships to employers.

Thus, he warns, inferring and evaluating employer behavior "from aggregate data is misleading." G. T. Milkovich, "Wage Discrimination and Comparable Worth," *Industrial and Labor Relations Report*, Vol. 19, No. 2 (Spring 1982), p. 9.

demographic factors are introduced into the analysis.[21] No studies undertaken thus far, however, have effectively quantified and controlled for all of these factors, and those that have been taken into account do not eliminate the differential entirely. As the Census Bureau has recognized:

> Although it is possible to quantify variables such as work experience and educational attainment, it is more difficult to measure differences in hiring and promotion practices. Social scientists have not been able to measure directly the possible effects of sex discrimination on women's earnings. After all measurable variables are included in an equation to account for earnings difference between women and men, there is almost always a residual difference that cannot be explained. Some researchers argue that this residual difference may arise partly from sex discrimination although data collected by the Census Bureau can neither prove nor disprove this assertion.[22]

Discrimination As An Explanation Of The Pay Gap

We are thus left with two important unanswered questions. Is the residual pay gap—that which is not accounted for in the various statistical analyses—the result of sex discrimination? If so, what portion is the result of discrimination by employers, as opposed to discrimination in education and other societal forms of sex discrimination?

It may be argued, of course, that discrimination is discrimination, and there is no need to pause for a more careful examination of the problem. But the corollary of this approach is the questionable proposition that all discrimination, regardless of its source, can be remedied by regulating the employment process. Affirmative action programs have done much to offset and remedy some of the effects of societal discrimination through constructive uses of the employment mechanism. But even such programs are not without limitations. And to the extent that we depend on affirmative action to offset discrimination which occurs apart from the employment process, we are leaving the basic

---

[21]Testimony by Commissioner of Bureau of Labor Statistics, Joint Hearings on Pay Equity before the Subcommittees on Human Resources, Civil Service, and Compensation and Employee Benefits of the Committee on Post Office and Civil Service, House of Representatives, 97th Cong., 2d Sess., Sept. 16, 1982, pp. 51-62.

[22]Statement of C. Lewis Kincannon, Deputy Director, Census Bureau, before the U.S. Congress Joint Economic Committee Hearings on Women in the Workforce, Nov. 9, 1983.

sources of such discrimination unremedied. The law has not been interpreted, and cannot be expected, to require employers to provide remedies for the effects of discriminatory attitudes perpetuated by parents, peer groups, school officials or other institutions in our society. It would appear to be more prudent and effective to pursue the broadly accepted goal of pay equity by applying employment discrimination remedies to wage differentials caused by employment practices, while seeking to identify other appropriate solutions for portions of the pay gap that are attributable to other causes.[23]

One of the significant factors contributing to today's pay gap is the impact of past differences in educational opportunities for males and females. The National Advisory Council on Women's Educational Programs has observed that:

> Before Title IX [of the Education Amendments of 1972], many educational institutions and programs used quotas or other systems that placed discriminatory numerical limitations on admission of females. . . . Many of these . . . admissions practices, although not always stated as written policy, required higher standards for women applicants. . . . Some admissions practices of the past were based on traditional attitudes about the "proper" place of women.[24]

Recent dramatic changes in the educational picture foretell a future narrowing of the pay gap. For example, in 1971-1972, 9% of the first professional medical degrees were earned by women. By 1979-80, that number had climbed to 23%. Even greater increases were seen in the number of women earning first professional degrees in law (from 7% in 1971-72 to 31% in 1979-80) and veterinary degrees (from 9% in 1971-72 to 33% in 1979-

---

[23]In reviewing social science literature about earnings differences, it is important to keep in mind that writers sometimes use the term "discrimination" in a very broad sense without respect to the specific meaning of that term in defining illegal conduct under our equal employment laws. One such example is the National Academy of Sciences report discussed in later chapters. Title VII of the Civil Rights Act, as interpreted by the Supreme Court in the case of *County of Washington v. Gunther*, 452 U.S. 161 (1981), prohibits pay differentials which are the result of *intentional* sex discrimination. The NAS committee, after examining literature on pay differences, observed that "there is substantial discrimination in pay," but then immediately added that "discrimination, as the term is used in this report, does not imply intent but refers only to outcome." *Women, Work, and Wages*, p. 91.

[24]"Title IX: The Half Full, Half Empty Glass," National Advisory Council on Women's Educational Programs (Fall 1981), p. 25.

80).[25] It may also be noted that the number of women earning doctoral degrees increased significantly from 1972 to 1980, but many of these degrees continue to be in traditional fields of study.

> Although women made gains in agriculture, architecture, business and management, and engineering, the greatest number of women are still receiving degrees in fields that have traditionally attracted the largest numbers of women, such as education and social sciences.[26]

While recent achievements in education are encouraging, they serve to emphasize that today's pay gap is a phenomenon that goes far beyond the workplace. We can and do demand that employment policies not be the source of sex or race discrimination. But, is it either reasonable or realistic to expect that our equal employment policies should bear the burden of eliminating every manifestation of sex and race discrimination in our society?

---

[25]*Ibid*, p. 31. Data showing the increasing number of women in many predominantly-male occupations are set forth in Chapter Eight.
[26]*Ibid*, pp. 29-30.

Chapter Four

EXISTING LAWS AND UNANSWERED LEGAL QUESTIONS

In the effort to eliminate employment discrimination, federal, state and local governments have enacted a variety of laws and regulations to promote equal employment opportunities. These laws have generally been designed to assure that factors such as sex and race will not be used by employers to differentiate among individuals, either in the selection of candidates for hire or promotion, or in the establishment of pay rates and other conditions of employment for those who have been selected. At the same time, these existing laws have been designed to accomplish their objectives with a minimum of governmental interference in the economy and in the management of employers' business operations. Consequently, direct government intervention in the setting of pay rates has generally been avoided in the United States.

The federal government did experiment briefly with wage controls during World War II and again in the early 1970's, but these programs were regarded as extraordinary wartime measures.[1] Also, both federal and state governments enforce minimum wage and overtime laws and prevailing wage requirements for certain classes of government contractors. Otherwise, existing laws generally leave the setting of pay rates open to free market economic forces and collective bargaining, subject only to the

---

[1] The World War II program administered by the National War Labor Board is discussed in the context of the legal framework of comparable worth in *Comparable Worth: Issues and Alternatives*, ed., E. Livernash (1980), pp. 205-212.

requirement that the rates thus established not be based on sex, race or other prohibited, discriminatory considerations.

Existing Wage Discrimination Laws

Wage discrimination on the basis of sex is prohibited by existing federal laws.[2] These laws are designed generally to assure equal access to higher paying jobs and the payment of equal wages for the performance of the same work. Specifically, under laws such as Title VII of the 1964 Civil Rights Act and the Equal Pay Act, women *cannot* be:

—denied equal pay for equal work;
—intentionally paid differently than men because of their sex;
—discriminated against in initial job assignments;
—intentionally segregated into "women's" jobs;
—denied the right to apply for any jobs, particularly higher paying jobs often performed by males;
—denied training, transfers, promotions or any other job opportunities because of their sex; or
—subjected to intentional job evaluation manipulations that downgrade women's pay because of their sex.

Whenever an employer is shown to have violated these laws, back pay and wage adjustment remedies can be ordered.

Women workers also are benefited by the federal government's affirmative action requirements for federal contractors. Contractors are required to evaluate their workforces to determine whether women are "underutilized" in any job categories. If they are, the contractor must establish goals and timetables, make good faith efforts to find women for those job categories and to

---

[2]For the sake of brevity, the discussion in this chapter focuses on federal laws. It is important to be aware, however, that some forty-three states and numerous local governments also have laws prohibiting discrimination in private sector employment. Most are patterned generally after Title VII of the federal Civil Rights Act of 1964, and virtually all prohibit discrimination in compensation on the basis of race or sex. Equal pay is specifically required in some thirty-six states, either as part of the general employment discrimination law or under a separate state statute. Unlike state laws in many other subject areas, these state employment discrimination laws are not superseded or preempted by the similar federal legislation. Rather, the state and federal requirements overlap, and employers are obliged to comply with whichever is most stringent. Thus, state and local governments have the power to impose legal requirements and remedies that go beyond those of federal law in the area of employment discrimination.

hire them in numbers proportionate to their availability in the labor market.[3] In addition, United States Department of Labor regulations have established for all federal construction contractors a nationwide hiring goal for women of 6.9 percent.[4] Failure to make good faith efforts to meet these obligations can result in sanctions, including cancellation of existing contracts or debarment from bidding on additional contracts.

Application of these laws and regulations provides the basis for attacking the practices of any employer that intentionally discriminates against women. Some advocates of comparable worth have argued that the situation faced by women today is the equivalent of the "separate but equal" status accorded to blacks earlier in this century.[5] This argument, of course, glosses over an important distinction. The fundamental inequity in the "separate but equal" predicament of blacks was that they were denied access to the schools attended by whites and were denied the opportunity to compete for the same jobs sought by whites. Existing employment discrimination laws require both that women be given equal access to all jobs, including those traditionally held by males, and that women receive the same pay as men for performing those jobs.

Although the Equal Pay Act and Title VII are not new statutes, issues of sex-based wage discrimination have not previously received the attention they are receiving today. When our equal employment opportunity laws initially took effect, there were other issues of employment discrimination which necessarily had priority. Questions about race and sex discrimination in hiring and promotion were among the first to demand attention. As the former Chair of the Equal Employment Opportunity Commission observed, the question of wage discrimination and pay equity was "bound to be the last to ripen. It is easily the most difficult issue ever to arise under the statute, and in a very real sense, it was inappropriate to go very far in trying to develop it

---

[3]Executive Order 11246, 30 Fed. Reg. 12319 (1965), *as amended by* 32 Fed. Reg. 14303 (1967) and 43 Fed. Reg. 46501 (1978). *See also*, Nelson, Opton & Wilson, *Wage Discrimination and the "Comparable Worth" Theory in Perspective*, 13 Mich. J.L. Ref. 231, 298 (1980).
[4]45 Fed. Reg. 65979 and 45 Fed. Reg. 85750.
[5]See Statement of Winn Newman, counsel for plaintiffs in *AFSCME v. State of Washington*, during Joint Hearings on Pay Equity before Subcommittees of the Committee on Post Office and Civil Service, House of Representatives, 97th Cong. 2d Sess., Sept. 16, 1982, pp. 146-47.

before simpler concepts under the statute were developed.''[6] As the discussion in this chapter will show, the law in this area is just now being developed. Many unanswered legal questions remain to be settled. In terms of the overall history of Title VII, the Supreme Court's landmark decision in the *Gunther* case is a relatively recent event and we are merely at the threshold of post-*Gunther* enforcement of the statute.

The Equal Pay Act

The debate today involves whether these existing laws should be expanded to require not simply equal pay for equal work, but also equal pay for work which is different in content, but somehow determined to be of comparable value to the employer or the community as a whole. Whether existing laws can properly be interpreted to include a requirement of equal pay for jobs of comparable worth has been the subject of much attention in the pay equity debate. A brief review of the legal arguments involved is helpful in understanding the other issues in that debate.

In 1963, Congress passed the Equal Pay Act, which states that an employer may not pay employees of one sex less than employees of the opposite sex for performing "equal work"— that is, work of substantially similar content requiring equal skill, effort and responsibility, and which is performed under similar working conditions—unless the difference in pay is based on a difference in seniority, merit, quantity or quality of production, or some other "factor other than sex".[7] In the debates preceding enactment of the Equal Pay Act, Congress specifically rejected a proposed legal standard that would have required an employer to pay the same wage to workers performing work of "comparable character" on jobs requiring "comparable skills". Congress expressed concern that this latter standard was vague, and

---

[6]See remarks of Eleanor Holmes Norton in *Comparable Worth: A Symposium on the Issues and Alternatives*, Proceedings of Nov. 21, 1980, Washington, D.C., p. 50. Chair Norton has noted that when she came to the EEOC in 1977, this issue of wage discrimination and pay equity was largely unknown, and that in prior years the Commission had led the fight for equal employment opportunity by focusing on many other issues ranging from pregnancy discrimination to the formulation of job-related standards for employee selection. See testimony presented at Joint Hearings on Pay Equity before Subcommittees on Human Resources, Civil Service, Compensation and Employee Benefits of the Committee on Post Office and Civil Service, House of Representatives, 97th Cong., 2d Sess., Sept. 16, 1982, p. 40.
[7]29 U.S.C. § 206(d)(1).

gave too much enforcement latitude to courts and administrative agencies.[8]

The Equal Pay Act has been interpreted by the courts to prohibit employers not only from paying women less than men working in *identical* jobs, but also from paying women less when they work in jobs that are *substantially the same* as jobs held by men.[9] Thus, employers cannot evade their responsibility under the Equal Pay Act by drawing overly-technical distinctions between jobs or by resorting to subterfuges, such as giving different titles to jobs that are essentially the same or assigning some inconsequential extra duties to men in an attempt to justify paying them more than women who do basically the same work. Nor have the courts allowed employers to pay women less than they would pay men for performing the same work simply because the employers were able to find women who were willing to work for lower wages. A difference in the prevailing market rates for workers' labor based on the sex of the individual workers has never been considered a legitimate "factor other than sex" that would justify pay differences under the Equal Pay Act.[10]

Title VII of the Civil Rights Act of 1964

One year after passing the Equal Pay Act, the same Congress in its second session enacted Title VII of the Civil Rights Act of 1964, which broadly prohibits discrimination based on race, color, religion, sex or national origin in all phases of employment, including compensation. There was little discussion of pay discrimination in the debates preceding Title VII's passage, and almost no discussion of sex discrimination. At the last minute, however, some concern was expressed in the Senate that Title VII's broad language might be read to override the limitations so carefully written into the Equal Pay Act the year before. To

---

[8]The motion to substitute the "equal work" standard for the "comparable" work language of the bill was introduced in the House by Representative Katharine St.George, who expressed concern that the term " 'comparable' opens up great vistas. It gives tremendous latitude to whoever is to be the arbitrator in these disputes." 108 Cong. Rec. 14767. Numerous other members of Congress echoed the view that a "comparable work" standard was too vague and would place too much authority in the hands of the government enforcement agencies and courts. See generally, *Comparable Worth: Issues and Alternatives*, ed., E. Livernash (1980), pp. 212-221.
[9]*E.g.*, *Schultz v. Wheaton Glass Co.*, 421 F.2d 259 (3d Cir.), *cert. denied*, 398 U.S. 905 (1970).
[10]*Corning Glass Works v. Brennan*, 417 U.S. 188, 207-08 (1974); *Hodgson v. Brookhaven General Hospital*, 436 F.2d 719 (5th Cir. 1970).

31

avoid this unintended result, Congress added a provision known as the "Bennett Amendment" to Title VII.[11] That amendment provides that it is not unlawful under Title VII for an employer to differentiate in wage rates between men and women "if such differentiation is authorized by [the Equal Pay Act]."[12]

Title VII plainly extends the legal ban against pay discrimination to cover discrimination based on race, religion and national origin as well as that based on sex. It is not yet clear, though, to what extent Title VII goes beyond the Equal Pay Act in terms of allowing claims of pay discrimination involving jobs that are different in content.

The first attempts to broaden the interpretation of existing federal law to prohibit pay differences to members of one sex who perform jobs that were not "equal", but nevertheless were "comparable" in value to the job performed by members of the other sex, began in the late 1970's. Several lawsuits seeking court approval of comparable worth were filed under Title VII. In the leading case, *County of Washington v. Gunther*, the U.S. Supreme Court in a 5-4 decision held that the broader sex discrimination provisions of Title VII could be used to prohibit employers from *intentionally* paying female employees less because of their sex than male employees who were performing *different* work.[13] But the Court noted that its decision was not based upon the "controversial concept of 'comparable worth'." The Court's decision left

---

[11]42 U.S.C. § 2000e-2(h).

[12]The meaning of the Bennett Amendment was widely debated until 1981 when the Supreme Court rendered a final interpretation in *County of Washington v. Gunther*, 452 U.S. 161. Many authorities, including Senator Bennett who drafted the amendment, had maintained that it was intended to limit sex-based wage discrimination claims under Title VII to cases involving denials of equal pay for equal work, thus preserving the standard Congress had adopted in the Equal Pay Act. 111 Cong. Rec. 13359. The Supreme Court, however, ruled by a 5-4 vote that claims of sex-based wage discrimination under Title VII are not limited to claims of unequal pay for equal work. The Court held that the Bennett Amendment was intended merely to incorporate into Title VII the Equal Pay Act's four affirmative defenses, which permit pay differentials based on (1) seniority, (2) merit, (3) quantity or quality of production, or (4) any other factor other than sex. 452 U.S. at 171.

[13]452 U.S. 161 (1981). The *Gunther* case involved a claim by female jail matrons who sought to compare their work to that of male corrections officers. The jobs were found by the Court to be different, with the corrections officers having more responsibility. The employer had conducted a study that concluded that the matrons should be paid 95% as much as the male officers, but then proceeded to pay the matrons at only 70% of the officers' wage rate. The Supreme Court held that if it could be proved that this disparity was the result of sex discrimination, then a violation of Title VII could be established. The Supreme Court sent the case back to the trial court to permit the plaintiffs to introduce evidence of such discrimination, if any existed. A settlement was then reached, however, before any further evidence was produced.

it unclear whether or how suits that were based on that concept could be brought under Title VII. The dissenting opinion would have rejected the theory outright and stated that "we should not be surprised that the Court [majority] disassociates itself with the entire notion of comparable worth."[14]

A number of lower court decisions have expressed skepticism about comparable worth under existing law. One district court judge stated a court "cannot, and will not, evaluate different jobs and determine their worth to an employer or to society and then, on that basis alone, determine whether [the law] has been violated."[15] The Court of Appeals for the Tenth Circuit in Denver refused to enter the "whole new world" of ignoring the market place in setting wages and "cross job description lines" to compare "entirely different skills."[16] Likewise, the Eighth Circuit said that it could not construe the law "to abrogate the laws of supply and demand or other economic principles that determine wage rates for various kinds of work."[17]

More recently, the Fifth Circuit was faced with a claim by a plaintiff who sought to compare her job with a different job held by a man who received a higher salary. The plaintiff claimed that the dissimilarity in duties did not justify the extent of the difference in the salaries. The court rejected the claim, noting that such a claim "would have the courts make an essentially subjective assessment of the value of the differing duties and responsibilities of the positions. . . ."[18] The court concluded that it is not the province of the courts to value the relative worth of differing duties and responsibilities and that such a claim does not fit within the cause of action delineated by the Supreme Court in *Gunther*.

---

[14]452 U.S. at 204. The majority opinion, in stressing that the claim in *Gunther* was not based on "comparable worth," emphasized the narrowness of the question before the Court. 452 U.S. at 166.

[15]*Power v. Barry County*, 539 F. Supp. 721, 726-27 (W.D. Mich. 1982). *See also, Connecticut State Employees Association v. State of Connecticut*, 31 Empl. Prac. Dec. (CCH) 33,528 (D. Conn. 1983), where the court stated that "a cause of action based exclusively on a theory of comparable worth would not be cognizable under Title VII. This Court will not engage in a subjective comparison of the intrinsic worth of various dissimilar jobs."

[16]*Lemons v. County of Denver*, 620 F.2d 228, 229 (10th Cir. 1980).

[17]*Christensen v. State of Iowa*, 563 F.2d 353, 356 (8th Cir. 1977). *See also Briggs v. City of Madison*, 536 F. Supp. 435 (W.D. Wis. 1982), discussed in detail in Chapter Five.

[18]*Plemer v. Parsons-Gilbane*, 713 F.2d 1127, 1134 (5th Cir. 1983). The court did accept plaintiff's alternative claim in which she compared her salary to the higher salary received by her successor who apparently performed identical work. By showing that she was paid less for performing the same job, she had established a prima facie case under the Equal Pay Act.

The Washington State Case

The much publicized case of *AFSCME v. State of Washington*[19] has often been described as a decision approving comparable worth. The trial judge in that case, however, did not impose on the State a comparable worth system of his own design. Rather, he held the State responsible to pay its employees in accordance with the State's own comparable worth studies. Those studies, initially commissioned by the Governor in 1974 at the request of officials of the state employees' union, concluded that there was a disparity in pay between predominantly male and predominantly female job classifications. The State's subsequent failure fully to correct this disparity was viewed by the trial judge as intentional sex discrimination, and at this writing the State faces a potential back pay award totaling hundreds of millions of dollars.[20]

While the *State of Washington* decision does not formally involve judicial imposition of comparable worth as a remedy in a Title VII sex discrimination case, it does raise serious questions about the appropriate use of job evaluation studies by employers. As is discussed in detail in Chapter Six, because job evaluation is not a scientific process, many experts have expressed doubts about the validity of using job evaluation as a mechanism for proving wage discrimination in the context of legal proceedings. An unfortunate consequence of the potential multi-million dollar verdict against the State of Washington is that it may actually make employers reluctant to conduct otherwise useful job evaluation studies for fear that the valuations suggested in the study will be elevated to the level of legal certainties and any disparities between those valuations and rates actually paid will automatically be treated as evidence of discrimination.

The Developing Law

The trial judge in the *State of Washington* case observed that the case was actually very similar to the situation in *Gunther*, where the employer had paid the men's jobs, but not the women's

---

[19]578 F. Supp. 846, 33 Fair Empl. Prac. Cas. (BNA) 808 (W.D. Wash. 1983).
[20]The trial court's decision in the *State of Washington* case has been appealed to the United States Court of Appeals for the Ninth Circuit.

34

jobs, at the rate the employer's job study had suggested. As indicated above, the Supreme Court in *Gunther* held that, if it could be proved that intentional sex discrimination was the reason for such difference in treatment, the women would be entitled to a remedy. In the *State of Washington* case, the judge concluded that the State had, in fact, acted with discriminatory intent in failing to eliminate the wage disparities indicated by its study. The judge's approach underscores the fact that those cases in which plaintiffs with wage bias claims have prevailed thus far have generally been cases in which the court sought to base its ruling on a finding that the employer committed some discriminatory practice, apart from the alleged under-valuation of jobs.

Where such a discriminatory practice is found, of course, the plaintiff can prevail without the court expanding existing law to encompass claims for comparable worth. For example, in *Taylor v. Charley Brothers Co.*,[21] the trial court did refer to the "inherent worth" of certain jobs, but neither the essential facts of the case nor the court's final ruling focus on the valuation of different jobs. Rather, the primary issue involved a series of employment practices which have long been recognized to be intentional sex discrimination. Specifically, the employer's warehousing operation was separated into two departments, with Department 1 employing only male workers and Department 2 employing all of the female workers. In a traditional Equal Pay Act analysis, the court found numerous jobs in which women in Department 2 were performing substantially equal work in almost identical jobs to men in Department 1, but the women were receiving less pay. Moreover, the court found that Charley Brothers had violated Title VII by classifying jobs into departments according to the sex of the individual holding the job, by segregating women within a single department within the company, and by refusing to consider women applicants—no matter what their qualifications—for openings in Department 1. Against this background of intentional sex discrimination, the court also noted that there were women in Department 2 who performed jobs which, while not identical to jobs in Department 1, were very similar in that the jobs in both departments were "characteristic of laborer's work requiring little skill, education or experi-

[21] 25 Fair Empl. Prac. Cas. (BNA) 602 (W.D. Pa. 1981).

ence."[22] With respect to these jobs, the court found that the company was paying the women substantially less than the men in Department 1, not because the jobs in Department 2 were inherently worth less, but because the jobs were in a department populated solely by women.[23]

Similarly, in another wage discrimination case, *Melani v. Board of Higher Education*,[24] the plaintiffs presented evidence to show that women hired on the instructional staff of a university were assigned substantially lower ranks, and thus lower salaries, than men hired with similar qualifications and characteristics. In contrast, in *Lemons*, a pre-*Gunther* case noted above, where the sole issue was valuation of different jobs, and where the employer had committed none of the practices traditionally defined as discrimination, the court rejected the plaintiffs' allegation of sex-based wage bias.

Neither the decided cases nor the general debate over comparable worth have yet shed much light on some crucial legal issues. Specifically, the courts have provided minimal guidance on how claims alleging wage discrimination, other than equal pay for equal work claims, can be proved.[25] The Supreme Court's

---

[22] 25 Fair Empl. Prac. Cas. at 613.

[23] 25 Fair Empl. Prac. Cas. at 614. The *Charley Brothers* opinion, which was issued before the *Gunther* decision, does not cite any case law. Another example of a case where the district court nominally endorsed comparable worth, but decided the case on other grounds is *EEOC v. Hay Associates*, 545 F. Supp. 1064 (E.D. Pa. 1982). The court decided plaintiff's wage discrimination claim as an "equal work" claim under the Equal Pay Act, but suggested that a "comparable worth" claim would be permitted under Title VII. The court simply cited *Gunther* to support this suggestion. 545 F. Supp. at 1083. As noted above, however, the Supreme Court in *Gunther* took care to explain that its decision was not based on a theory of comparable worth. *See also Moseley v. Kellwood Co.*, 27 Empl. Prac. Dec. (CCH) 32,348 (E.D. Mo. 1981) ("Even if this Court were to apply a 'comparable worth' theory to this case, which *Gunther* did not endorse but which plaintiff has suggested, there is no basis for a conclusion that plaintiff was underpaid by defendant.").

[24] 561 F. Supp. 769 (S.D.N.Y. 1983).

[25] In several cases not involving claims of equal pay for comparable worth, the courts have offered interesting insights into the effect of Title VII after *Gunther*. For example, in *Bartlet v. Berlitz School of Languages*, 698 F.2d 1003 (9th Cir. 1983), female plaintiffs who worked as school directors filed claims under Title VII charging that the company paid them less than it paid male directors who performed substantially equal work at other schools. Berlitz argued that under the Equal Pay Act comparisons of wages were limited to employees performing equal work *within the same establishment*. The court ruled, however, that the "single establishment" limitation of the Equal Pay Act does not preclude the plaintiffs from bringing a wage discrimination claim under Title VII. In another post-*Gunther* case, *Kouba v. Allstate Insurance Co.*, 691 F.2d 873 (9th Cir. 1983), the court of appeals reversed a finding of sex discrimination by a lower court and offered a thorough discussion of how the "factor other than sex" defense of the Equal Pay Act is to be interpreted in Title VII litigation.

Gunther decision left this task to the lower courts, but those courts have only begun to address the issue thus far. Nor have proponents of comparable worth suggested acceptable alternatives.

At the root of the problem is the question of what mechanism or methodology is to be used to determine that two jobs of different content are comparable in value. The traditional mechanism for establishing pay rates in our economy has been the labor market. If comparable worth is adopted, it seems obvious that some standards of comparison would be required. What would such standards be, and who would be responsible for developing them? Are there common factors of job content applicable to all jobs? If so, how are these factors determined? How are values placed on such factors? How will wide variations in the value of particular jobs to different employers, or to the same employer at different times, be reconciled? Will assessments of job worth be made by some governmental agency? Or, will they be made by employers, subject to the review of courts or administrative agencies? It would be imperative under a comparable worth scheme that standards be developed to assure that these subjective assessments would not be simply arbitrary evaluations.

If the law is to impose some new system for making wage determinations, another question that immediately arises is how that system will relate to the market forces of supply and demand, which presumably will continue to operate. Can a totally market-free system be devised? If so, how will job values be established? Whose value standards will apply? How much government intervention into the economy would this approach entail? And how would such a policy affect companies that operate at or near the margin, as is true of many companies that provide employment to the least skilled and least experienced workers in the labor force?

Fundamental to the concept of comparable worth is acceptance of the proposition that some entity will make a determination of the worth of each job. Today such determinations are made by employers individually or through collective bargaining, governed primarily by market forces. Under comparable worth, they would be made by third parties or would be subject to third party approval and would be governed primarily by assessments of job content. To be enforceable, the determinations would necessarily have to meet basic standards of legal certainty. They would have to be determined by procedures incorporating rules of evidence and standards of proof and affording due process to the parties involved. Consequently the unanswered legal questions cannot be avoided or ignored. To place those questions in perspective, the next two chapters will explore first the role of the labor market in determining wage rates and then the characteristics of the job evaluation techniques commonly practiced in U.S. industry.

Chapter Five

THE ROLE OF THE MARKET
IN PAY SETTING

In any discussion of the comparable worth theory, it is important to keep in mind that the relative "worth" of any particular item is inevitably a matter of values. For commercial purposes, the worth of oranges, diamonds or automobiles is the composite of individual values and choices which are reflected in the system we call the market. None of these market prices purports to represent a precise universal "worth" for these particular products in comparison with the intrinsic "worth" of other goods. Each market price, however, does provide a rough valuation which permits commercial transactions to be carried out.

In a similar way, the series of values and choices represented by the labor market works to set the price that is paid for different jobs. Human beings are not mere commodities, but the wage an individual receives in exchange for his or her labor is nevertheless a price that reflects the conglomeration of the supply of individuals with similar skills and the worth of those skills to the various employers who need them. Diamonds command a higher price in the marketplace than oranges because they are less plentiful, not because they are more useful. A skilled football place kicker can earn more than a skilled welder, not because kicking field goals is necessarily more difficult or more valuable to society than welding, but because fewer people have perfected that particular skill. Oranges are unlikely ever to be priced as high as diamonds, or welders as high as place kickers, but a sudden shortage in the supply of either oranges or welders will cause noticeable increases in their market prices.

Thus, just as with the prices of commercial products, labor market values react to forces of supply and demand, and the market value of a particular job can change over a period of time and need not remain in a static relationship to other job values. It is the differential between the wages paid for different jobs that is of primary concern in the comparable worth debate.

The committee of the National Academy of Sciences which studied the issue of comparable worth at great length under a contract with the Equal Employment Opportunity Commission acknowledged in its final report that "no universal standard of job worth exists."[1] This lack of any universal standard for computing intrinsic worth occurs, according to the NAS committee, "because any definition of the 'relative worth' of jobs is in part a matter of values and because, even for a particular definition, problems of measurement are likely."[2]

Basic Market Factors Influencing Wage Determination

While it is not the purpose of this paper to examine in depth the various theories of wage determination, it is helpful to keep in mind some concepts that are basic to our economic system. First, ours is not a rigidly administered system where jobs are assigned and wages determined by some central authority:

> [T]he labor market is the only device we have for sorting out many millions of workers with varying skills and interests among the multitude of different jobs in the economy. Any attempt to do this by administrative methods, in addition to encroaching on personal liberty, would be hopelessly cumbersome and inefficient. Even communist countries . . . rely mainly on wage inducements in the market to secure a desirable allocation of the labor force.[3]

Second, the market forces that affect pay rates are constantly changing. Within a labor market, the demand for labor and the supply of labor interact to determine how many individuals will be employed in each occupation and how much they will be paid at a given time and place. Put simply, a worker chooses to be

---

[1] *Women, Work, and Wages*, p. 94.
[2] *Ibid.*
[3] L. G. Reynolds, *Labor Economics and Labor Relations* (7th ed. 1978), pp. 13-14.

40

employed in a certain area or at a certain type of job, and an employer desires to hire employees with certain skills or qualifications. "These preferences vary from person to person and from time to time for the same person, and when they are totaled," they constitute a market which is "an area with indistinct geographical and occupational limits within which certain workers customarily seek to offer their services and certain employers to purchase them."[4]

Employee Preferences

Employee choice is a significant factor underlying differentials in pay rates. Because U.S. workers have substantial freedom to choose the jobs they wish to perform, there may be an oversupply of workers for some jobs as opposed to other jobs which fewer workers find attractive or for which not as many have gained the necessary experience, seniority, education or other qualifications.

> Speaking . . . generally, we can say . . . that both jobs and people are highly differentiated in their respective natures. People differ in their capacities for potential service. They vary in skill and experience, in their willingness to take risks, in their strength and their willingness to put forth physical effort, and in their tastes for various kinds of jobs. In a free society, these differences, which find expression through labor supply, become one of the main sources for wage structure or for relative wages. The other source, of course, is demand.[5]

In discussing "employee choice" as a factor in the operation of the labor market, it is important to recognize that this term is used to express the fact that individuals each have their own unique tastes, preferences, values, and wants which they will seek to satisfy. The collective impact of these individual choices has consequences for the labor market. Thus, to understand the market, it is important to appreciate the role of these individual choices. The use of the term "choice" does not mean, however, that there are no limitations which influence these individual

---

[4]C. Kerr, "The Balkanization of Labor Markets" in E. W. Bakke, et al., *Labor Mobility and Economic Opportunity* (1954), pp. 92-93.
[5]G. Hildebrand, "The Market System," in *Comparable Worth: Issues and Alternatives*, ed., E. Livernash (1980), p. 86.

decisions. Individuals "confront an environment which is external to themselves and which contains constraints which interfere with their want satisfaction. Because of these constraints, no individual is able to achieve all of his or her wants or desires. . . ."[6] More often than not, individuals are faced with the "choice" of achieving one objective at the cost of sacrificing another. "Thus individuals are forced to choose" and to "make the best choices, given their tastes and preferences and the costs which they face."[7] For the purpose of our discussion here, the significance of the "employee choice" factor is not that it is a factor which the individual is entirely free to control, but rather that it is a factor over which the employer has no control.

In understanding how individual preferences are exercised, it is important to remember that occupations differ in numerous ways, such as in the costs and time required to learn the occupation, the pleasantness or unpleasantness of the work and the workplace, the social esteem enjoyed by those in the job, the regularity of employment and the probability or possibility of success or failure. The labor market process functions by allowing the interaction of many such factors:

> Employers . . . compete on the basis of the relative agreeableness of the work that they offer and the pleasantness and convenience of the surroundings in which the work is done. Those employers who offer more stimulating work in more attractive settings may pay less than those who must compete in these dimensions at a disadvantage.

> By the same token, becoming qualified to work in some occupations costs more than becoming qualified to work in others. Becoming an accountant costs more than becoming an airline flight attendant. Hence, those employers who seek to attract accountants must offer salaries that compensate for these added costs of learning accountancy; otherwise, no one will bear these added

---

[6]D. Bellante and M. Jackson, *Labor Economics: Choice in Labor Markets* (1979), p. 2.
[7]*Ibid*. Professor Eli Ginzberg, in "The Theory of Occupational Choice," *The Development of Human Resources* (1966), p. 57, observes that "since occupational choice involves the balancing of a series of subjective elements with the opportunities and limitations of reality, the crystallization of occupational choice inevitably has the quality of a compromise."

costs to become accountants. Nor, at the wages of flight attendants, would many be attracted into medicine, dentistry and law.[8]

Some characteristics of jobs cannot be changed, others change only gradually, and still others experience rapid changes. Rates of pay are the most flexible element in the system.[9] How quickly such changes in market valuation (and thus in the resulting wage differentials) occur is a question likely to be answered differently by different economic theorists depending on their view of the market, but it cannot be disputed that such changes occur. For example:

> In the 1970s, . . . there was a marked narrowing in the differentials between highly educated white-collar and other workers. The ratio of the earnings of college graduates fell relative to high school graduates. The income of scientists, professors and related personnel dropped relative to factory workers. The prime reason for this is the rapid expansion in the supply of graduates in the seventies coupled with slackened growth of demand.[10]

Differing Views of Labor Markets

In a perfectly competitive labor market, purchasers and suppliers of labor possess complete information and total mobility, and the unfettered adjustment of supply and demand determines the wage of each worker.[11] But today's labor market is not perfectly competitive. As found in the National Academy of Sciences report on comparable worth,

---

[8]C. M. Lindsay and C. A. Shanor, "*County of Washington v. Gunther*: Economic and Legal Considerations for Resolving Sex-Based Wage Discrimination Claims," 1 *Supreme Court Economic Review* 185, 200-01, (1982).

[9]L. G. Reynolds, *Labor Economics and Labor Relations* (7th ed. 1978), p. 252. Differentials in competitive wages can serve to equalize the differences in occupations. For example, because jobs differ in their unpleasantness, wages may be used to attract individuals to certain less desirable work. But, as is noted in P. Samuelson, *Economics* (11th ed. 1980), p. 544, wage differentials also reflect certain differences among individual workers:

> Even in a hypothetically perfect auction market, where all the different categories of labor were priced by supply and demand, equilibrium would necessitate tremendous differentials in wages. This is because of the tremendous *qualitative* differentials among people—traceable to differences in environmental opportunity that go back to early life and to other individual differences—all of which lead to competitive wage differentials.

[10]R. Freeman, *Labor Economics* (2d ed. 1979), p. 90.

[11]G. Hildebrand, "The Market System," in *Comparable Worth: Issues and Alternatives*, ed., E. Livernash (1980), pp. 899-90.

workers rarely participate in the labor market with full information
or mobility, [and] are often not aware of all opportunities. . . .
Similarly, employers rarely have access to all possible employees
and are often constrained by custom, [collective bargaining] agree-
ments, and other factors.[12]

Because of this lack of perfect competition, the NAS committee
chose to base its analysis on the so-called "institutional" view
of labor markets. This view focuses on the importance of various
institutional rules which affect the relationship between the employer and the employee and which thus contribute to the market
structure. A seniority system, or rules established in response to
government regulations, are examples of such institutional rules.
This view of the market is in contrast to the conventional "neo-
classical" view of the market which focuses on the competitive
market created by individual choices and preferences.[13]

The NAS committee acknowledged that its "institutional"
view is not the only approach to analyzing a labor market. The
committee further admitted that its view emphasizes the relative
inflexibility of institutional features as a factor in determining
wages and working conditions. Thus, the NAS study conceded
that it began its analysis using a theory which views "labor
markets as inherently rigid and balkanized" and which "provides
a basis for viewing discrimination as an integral part of both
labor market processes and their outcomes."[14] The NAS report
recognized that in choosing to use the institutional view it was
choosing a view which is the subject of much controversy in
economics and sociology.[15] Having opted for this view, however,
the NAS then stressed that important changes have occurred in
the past two decades with respect to employment discrimination
against minorities and women. While such discrimination has
not been eliminated, NAS observed, its impact has been reduced
by legal, social, and political intervention.[16]

---

[12]*Women, Work, and Wages*, p. 45.
[13]The various theories describing the structure of labor markets are discussed in S. Levitan, et
al., *Human Resources and Labor Markets* (3d ed. 1981), pp. 96-120. See also the discussion
of structured and unstructured labor markets in G. Bloom and H. Northrup, *Economics of Labor
Relations* (9th ed. 1981) and C.Kerr, "The Balkanization of Labor Markets" in E.W. Bakke,
et al., *Labor Mobility and Economic Opportunity* (1954), pp. 93-109.
[14]*Women, Work, and Wages*, p. 62.
[15]*Ibid*, p. 45.
[16]*Ibid*, pp. 62-63.

Thus, even under the theory which views market forces as being most rigid and inflexible, it appears that our basic laws against discrimination have had a positive effect. These basic laws have not attempted to meddle with the action and reaction of market forces, but rather have provided that the race and sex of employees are not legitimate considerations in employment decisions by employers.

Societal Discrimination

Some advocates of comparable worth argue that societal discrimination against women has infected the labor market, causing lower wages for certain jobs traditionally occupied by women. Thus, in assigning responsibility for these low wages, they point to an alleged historical bias which is said to be operating in society and in the market generally, rather than to a direct act of sex discrimination by a particular employer. These advocates argue that an employer who relies on this "infected" market as a factor in setting wages discriminates against its employees on the basis of sex.

Under existing laws, the courts generally have found this argument unpersuasive. In *Briggs v. City of Madison*,[17] for example, a group of city nurses alleged that their work was undervalued by the City, and that the pay disparity could be traced to a traditional and long-accepted devaluation of the worth of jobs done primarily by women. The nurses did not prevail. Accepting the employer's defenses based on the market, Federal District Judge Barbara Crabb wrote:

> I find unpersuasive the basic premise that . . . any one possesses the intellectual tools and data base that would enable them to identify the extent to which the factor of discrimination has contributed to, or created, sex-segregated jobs, and to separate that factor from the myriad of nondiscriminatory factors that may have contributed to the same result.[18]

---

[17]536 F. Supp. 435 (W.D. Wis. 1982).

[18]536 F. Supp. at 444. The judge observed that the plaintiffs' argument about historical societal discrimination ignores a series of other potentially determinative factors, including the "historical reality that many of the jobs characterized by [the plaintiffs] as 'women's work' are jobs that have never been well-compensated, whether they have been filled by women or by men." *Id.* at 445.

In the court's view, there were significant nondiscriminatory factors contributing to the wage differential, such as

> familial and peer expectations, desire for part-time work or work with flexible hours, reluctance to pioneer in non-traditional fields, the absence of "role models" in non-traditional jobs, and lack of information about higher-paying jobs.[19]

The essential issue in *Briggs* was whether an employer who has committed no act of sex discrimination, but who has simply relied on the market in setting wages, is to be held liable under existing federal discrimination law. The court found that the remedial purpose of Title VII of the Civil Rights Act "is not so broad as to make employers liable for employment practices of others or for existing market conditions."[20] Advocates of comparable worth disagree with this conclusion and argue, in effect, that the premises of the law should be broadened, so as to make employers responsible for the effects of labor supply and demand conditions that impact more severely on one sex or race than another, regardless of whether the particular employer created those market conditions.

Discrimination Not Excused By Market Rates

In assessing such proposals to expand on existing laws, an important distinction should be kept in mind. That is, although Title VII has been interpreted to permit employers to rely upon the market in setting the wages for different jobs, the courts have *not* allowed the market to excuse discriminatory actions by employers. As detailed in the preceding chapter, the courts have refused to recognize lower market rates for workers of one sex as a legitimate factor justifying unequal pay for equal work under the Equal Pay Act. Similarly, market differences in the wage

---

[19]536 F. Supp. at 444-445 n.6.
[20]536 F. Supp. at 445. In *Wilkins v. University of Houston*, 654 F.2d 388 (5th Cir. 1981), *reversed and vacated on other grounds*, 103 S.Ct. 34 (1982), *affirmed on remand*, 695 F.2d 134 (5th Cir. 1983), the court implicitly recognized that the external labor market can be a legitimate consideration in determining levels of compensation. Although the court did not address the point directly, it did comment that faculty salaries in the schools of law and engineering were higher than salaries in other colleges within the University because of the higher market rates for people in those fields. In fact, the court found that the field within which a faculty member taught was the single most important factor affecting salaries. 654 F.2d at 402. Implicitly, the court approved the University's practice of taking these market differences into account in its pay system.

rates commanded by workers of different races or sexes will not excuse pay differentials under Title VII where substantially similar work is involved.[21] Moreover, existing law does not permit an employer who intentionally discriminates against minorities or women to hide behind a "market" defense. Indeed, as the Supreme Court has pointed out in *Arizona Governing Committee v. Norris*,[22] involving a pension plan that required women to make greater contributions than men,

> it is no defense that all annuities immediately available in the open market may have been based on sex-segregated actuarial tables.[23]

The key is whether the employer treats a woman in a manner that but for her sex would have been different.[24]

In other words, where the employer discriminates between men and women, the market can offer the employer no defense.[25] But where an employer sets a wage rate based upon a market rate for a particular job, without regard to the sex of the worker, the employer is simply exercising sound business judgment and is not discriminating.

In everyday terms, this means that the law does not permit an employer to pay a woman less because she is a woman, or because she is willing to do the work for less pay than the employer would pay a man for the same work. But the law does allow an employer to pay teachers less than truck drivers, so long as the difference in pay is because the jobs and the market for them are different and not because the sex of the workers is different.

A final point to be remembered about the labor market is that even where an employer has systematically evaluated different jobs, the effects of the market generally cannot be ignored. This point was demonstrated in graphic terms by the fact situation that produced one of the lawsuits cited in an earlier chapter. The employer, a state university, had evaluated certain predominantly-female clerical jobs as being at the same level as certain

---

[21]*See, e.g., Corning Glass Works v. Brennan*, 417 U.S. 188, 207-08 (1974).
[22]463 U.S. _____, 103 S.Ct. 3492 (1983).
[23]103 S.Ct. at 3500.
[24]*Los Angeles Department of Water & Power v. Manhart*, 435 U.S. 702, 710 (1978).
[25]*See, e.g., Taylor v. Charley Brothers Co.*, 25 FEP Cases 602 (W.D. Pa. 1981).

physical plant jobs held predominantly by males. The local job market, however, paid higher wages for physical plant jobs than the beginning pay under the university's system. When the university sought to hire employees, it found that it could hire workers for the clerical jobs at the evaluated level, but that it could not attract workers for physical plant jobs at that rate. To hire the workers it needed, the university was forced to increase the wage for the physical plant jobs. This supplementary wage was found to be nondiscriminatory by the court because the law does not require an employer to ignore the labor market in setting wage rates.[26]

One of the unresolved issues in the comparable worth debate is whether it reasonably can be *presumed*, simply because most clerical workers are females and most plant maintenance workers are males, that an employer's decision to pay the clericals less than maintenance workers is a sex-based decision. To support such an automatic presumption, the enforcement of equal employment opportunity laws in the United States would have to be modified in a fundamental way. Mechanisms for evaluating the relative worth of different jobs would have to become a basic part of our equal opportunity enforcement system. As indicated in the previous chapter, this would be a marked change from the existing system, which has operated by avoiding such subjective evaluations and by focusing instead on making the labor market as freely competitive as possible by eliminating sex and race as factors in employment decisions.

---

[26]See *Christensen v. State of Iowa*, 563 F.2d 353 (8th Cir. 1977).

Chapter Six

JOB EVALUATION—ITS LEGITIMATE ROLE AND ITS LIMITATIONS

In the controversy over the comparable worth theory, job evaluation has received much attention. The charge is sometimes made that many of the job evaluation systems currently used by employers operate in a biased fashion to undervalue the work done by employees in traditionally-female jobs. As the remarks by Representative Schroeder quoted in Chapter Two illustrate, advocates of comparable worth maintain that the development of bias-free evaluation systems could be the basis of a new equal employment opportunity enforcement scheme that would assure the realization of pay equity. Others argue that the issues cannot be dealt with so simply.

Types of Job Evaluation Systems

To understand the role of job evaluation in developing bias-free compensation systems, it is essential to recognize at the outset that even the most refined job evaluation techniques do not rise to the level of a science capable of producing absolute measurements of job worth. As the National Academy of Sciences report observed:

> The concept of intrinsic job worth—whether it exists, on what it should be based, whether there is a just wage—has been a matter of dispute for many centuries. We do not believe that the value—or worth—of jobs can be determined by scientific methods. Hier-

49

archies of job worth are always, at least in part, a reflection of values.[1]

There are, of course, many different kinds of job evaluation systems in use in U.S. industry and public sector employment.[2] At one end of the spectrum are simple, nonquantitative methods of comparing and ranking jobs within an organization, commonly known as "whole job" evaluation techniques.[3] At the opposite extreme are highly sophisticated, professionally-developed "factor" evaluation systems through which job content is analyzed in terms of various component factors, a point value is assigned to each factor on some common scale, and the point values of all factors are then combined, usually in accordance with a weighted formula (sometimes with the aid of computers), to yield an overall point total for each job which can then be compared with similarly-derived point values for other jobs.[4] Between these extremes is a wide variety of different systems, each typically having features of its own adapted to the specific needs and objectives of the particular employer.

Is Job Evaluation the Problem or the Solution?

Job evaluation systems can and do serve as valuable tools for managers in both private industry and the public sector. Properly designed and administered, a job evaluation system can facilitate the establishment of a pay scale that supports the objectives of the employing organization and is perceived as equitable by the employees. On the other hand, a job evaluation system that is designed or administered with bias can operate as

---

[1] *Women, Work, and Wages*, pp. 9-10.

[2] Job evaluation is a highly specialized area of expertise and is treated here only in very general terms. One of the best basic treatments of the subject may be found in *Elements of Sound Base Pay Administration*, 1981, published jointly by the American Society for Personnel Administration and The American Compensation Association. More extensive treatments of the issues may be found in D. Treiman, *Job Evaluation: An Analytic Review*, Interim Report to the Equal Employment Opportunity Commission, National Academy of Sciences, 1979; and D. Schwab, "Job Evaluation and Pay Setting: Concepts and Practices," *Comparable Worth: Issues and Alternatives*, ed., E. Livernash (1980).

[3] Common types of "whole job" evaluation systems include various simple ranking, classification and slotting techniques. See D. Treiman, *Job Evaluation: An Analytic Review*, pp. 2-3; *Elements of Sound Base Pay Administration*, pp. 7-8.

[4] One widely-known "factor" evaluation system is the "Hay System" developed by the Philadelphia-based consulting firm of Edward Hay Associates. Another is the National Metal Trades Association system.

an instrument of discrimination. Thus, it has been observed that job evaluation may be "both a potential cause and a solution to discrimination" in pay rates within a given company or organization.[5]

If it is shown that a job evaluation system has been intentionally designed or administered with bias against members of one sex or minority group, of course, existing laws would provide a remedy. Whether job evaluation can provide a workable means to implement a general legal mandate for comparable worth, however, is quite a different matter. As indicated in Chapter Four, Congress studied this precise issue in depth prior to the enactment of the Equal Pay Act.[6] Extensive Congressional hearings were held in 1962 and 1963 at which numerous expert witnesses described in detail the various types of job evaluation procedures used in U.S. industry.[7] Based on the evidence developed in those hearings, Congress reached two important conclusions.

On the one hand, Congress found that a job evaluation system can provide a valid, nondiscriminatory basis for an individual employer's decisions regarding pay rates for its own employees. Therefore, Congress made it clear that it did not intend to disturb the operation of bona fide job evaluation systems in American industry.[8]

On the other hand, the legislators concluded that job evaluation is not a sufficiently uniform or precise science to serve as the basis for a legislatively-imposed comparable worth standard for employers in general. Consequently, the Congress ultimately enacted a standard requiring equal pay for men and women performing "equal" work, but concluded that it would

---

[5]Remarks of Professor Donald Schwab in *Comparable Worth: A Symposium on the Issues and Alternatives*, proceedings of November 21, 1980, p. 27.

[6]The Equal Pay Act was enacted in 1963 as an amendment to the Fair Labor Standards Act, 29 U.S.C. § 206(d).

[7]The legislative history of the Equal Pay Act is discussed at length in *Comparable Worth: Issues and Alternatives*, ed., E. Livernash (1980), pp. 212-221. See also the discussions by the Supreme Court in *County of Washington v. Gunther*, 452 U.S. 160, 171 (1981), and *Corning Glass Works v. Brennan*, 417 U.S. 188, 199-200 (1974).

[8]As the Supreme Court noted in the *Corning Glass* case, after hearing testimony about the prevalence of job evaluation systems in U.S. industry, Congress added language to the Equal Pay Act to ensure that an employer's use of a bona fide job evaluation system would be considered a "factor other than sex" and would not be disrupted. 417 U.S. at 201. See also the discussion of legislative history in the dissenting opinion of Justice Rehnquist in *Gunther*. 452 U.S. at 184-189.

be neither feasible nor desirable to try to impose a legal standard requiring equal pay for "comparable" work.[9]

Job evaluation procedures have undoubtedly become somewhat more sophisticated in the past twenty years. But the conclusions Congress reached after studying job evaluation systems in 1962 and 1963 were essentially reconfirmed by the committee of the National Academy of Sciences in their 1981 study of the effect of job evaluation on women's wages, which has been referred to earlier. Again, after a thorough review of the state of the art of job evaluation, the NAS committee concluded that a comparable worth approach

> requires a generally acceptable standard of job worth and a feasible procedure for measuring the relative worth of jobs. In our judgment no universal standard of job worth exists, both because any definition of the "relative worth" of jobs is in part a matter of values and because, even for a particular definition, problems of measurement are likely.[10]

Basic Elements of Job Evaluation Systems

To appreciate why both the Congress and the NAS committee reached these conclusions and to assess their continuing validity, it may be useful to consider certain basic points about job evaluation. First, it is important to recognize that job evaluation systems exist in almost infinite varieties, and that no one system has ever been singled out as the best, or even as a suitable system for application in all circumstances. While there are certain more-or-less standard approaches to job evaluation, compensation experts generally agree that in practice, a system must be tailored to suit the particular circumstances, objectives and philosophies of the individual employer. Even when two different organizations nominally use the same system, their implementation of that system and the results it produces typically vary because of differences in the needs,

---

[9]Congress therefore rejected proposed language that would have required equal pay for men and women performing "work of comparable character on jobs the performance of which requires comparable skills." See H.R. 8898, 87th Cong., lst Sess., and H.R. 10226, 87 Cong., 2d Sess., reprinted in *Hearings Before the Select Subcommittee on Labor of the House Committee on Education and Labor on H.R. 8898, 10266*, Part I, 87 Cong. 2d Sess., pp. 2-10. Instead, the Equal Pay Act as enacted only requires equal pay for men and women performing *equal* work within the same establishment. 29 U.S.C. § 206(d).
[10]*Women, Work, and Wages*, p. 94.

goals and values of the two organizations. For this reason, consultants who assist employers in establishing such systems regularly stress the flexibility and adaptability of their recommended approaches.

Many widely-accepted job evaluation systems, of course, operate by comparing jobs in terms of the same four basic elements: skill, effort, responsibility and working conditions.[11] But this does not mean that the systems are therefore essentially all the same or that some standardized system based on those four elements would work for all employers. Each of the four elements is a broadly inclusive term that takes on different meanings in different employment contexts.[12]

"Skill," for example, may include such factors as education, training, experience and/or physical dexterity, as well as less tangible qualities such as interpretive, analytical or creative ability, leadership, judgment, facility for getting along with others, and so on. The particular aspects of "skill" that an organization will regard as valuable, and therefore compensable, will differ greatly depending not only on the nature of the job in question, but also on the goals, needs, and competitive position of the organization itself. Systems that are well-suited to evaluating the skill factors of jobs in some contexts have proved to be ineffective in others.

The same is true of "effort" (which may include not only physical demands but also mental stresses inherent in certain jobs), "responsibility" (which may include the consequences and accountability for possible errors, as well as such things as the amount and scope of supervision), and "working conditions" (which can take into account a broad range of factors including the location and environment in which the job is performed, the risks and hazards involved, the hours, the availability of benefits other than wages, and many others). Choosing the best methods of selecting and weighing particular aspects of skill, effort, responsibility, working conditions or other factors that an organization desires to treat as compensable

---

[11] In recognition of this fact, Congress incorporated the elements of skill, effort, responsibility and working conditions into the Equal Pay Act as standards for determining whether jobs of substantially similar content are in fact "equal" within the meaning of that statute.

[12] See *Elements of Sound Base Pay Administration, supra* note 2, p. 22.

involves a highly individualized exercise of managerial responsibility.[13]

Objectives of Job Evaluation Systems

A second, related point is that job evaluation and pay-setting systems generally are designed to serve multiple objectives for the employing organization. One reason why many employers adopt such systems is to try to achieve "internal equity" in pay rates—that is, a perception among employees that each job is fairly compensated in comparison with other jobs within the same organization. This concept of internal fairness is, of course, the focal point of "pay equity" proposals. But the perception of internal equity is *not the only* legitimate goal of a compensation system, and often not even the most important one. Equally significant for most organizations is maintaining "external competitiveness." This means paying enough to attract, retain and motivate employees with the skills and other qualities the organization needs, without incurring excessive labor costs. Failure to maintain external competitiveness can lead to the most serious internal consequences for employees, up to and including business failure and ultimate loss of jobs.

The levels of compensation that a given employer will deem appropriate for specific jobs will vary depending on such factors as the profitability of the business, the nature and extent of the competition in the particular industry and location or, in the case of a nonprofit organization or governmental unit, the limitations on the resources available to carry out its mission. Another important variable is the basic strategy the organization has adopted for achieving its business or operational goals. A company that

---

[13] As the NAS committee observed:

> [I]t must be recognized that there are no definitive tests of the "fairness" of the choice of compensable factors and the relative weights given to them. The process is inherently judgmental and its success in generating a wage structure that is deemed equitable depends on achieving a consensus about factors and their weights among employers and employees.

Women, Work, and Wages, p. 96. In D. Treiman, *Job Evaluation: An Analytic Review,* (1979), p. 7, the interim report prepared for the NAS committee, it was noted that

> it is choice of factors and factor weights that determines the relative ordering of jobs on the job worth scale. One set of factors and factor weights may produce a particular ordering of jobs while a different set of factors or a different weighting of factors may produce a quite different ordering.

54

seeks to trade on a reputation for superior quality products or services may be willing to pay its workers higher wages than its competitors pay theirs in order to attract and retain a more highly skilled workforce. Other companies may decide to keep wages as low as possible, even if it results in high employee turnover, so as to be able to compete by providing their products to the public at the lowest price.

Even within a single organization, different jobs may be affected by different managerial objectives. Experience and workforce stability may be viewed as essential in some phases of an operation, but unimportant in others. For example, a manufacturing firm might decide that it can operate effectively with inexperienced, relatively low-paid machine operators and assemblers as long as it has an expert staff of supervisors and quality controllers. Another company might adopt just the opposite strategy. One retail firm might stake its hopes on maintaining the most experienced sales force in its field, while keeping labor costs in its stock room, office and other areas at a minimum. Other firms might place greater emphasis on high quality customer service. A job evaluation system that focuses solely on internal equity is unlikely to produce pay scales that support each of these different objectives. Yet, if a job evaluation system is to serve as a valid tool for managers in a competitive economy, it must be designed and administered so as to facilitate whatever legitimate, nondiscriminatory business objectives and strategies the managers of the organization have decided to pursue.

Responsibility for Evaluating Jobs

This leads to a third fundamental point about job evaluation. That is, regardless of the type of system used, job evaluation and pay-setting necessarily involve decisions which, under our economic system, have traditionally been made exclusively by the managers of the employing organization, subject to employee consent or collective bargaining in appropriate circumstances. Each of these decisions, including the initial determination of what type of job evaluation system best suits the organization's purposes, the selection of the specific factors to be compensated and relative weights to be accorded them, and the ultimate application of the system to particular jobs, entails business judgments that must be harmonized with the basic goals, strategies and philosophy of the employing organization if job evaluation is to serve its essential purpose. Our society's few limited experiments with programs that have taken these decisions out of the employers' hands or subjected them to external controls— as for example the wage controls imposed by the federal government during the Nixon administration—have been extremely unpopular and widely-regarded as unsuccessful.[14]

The Subjective Nature of Job Evaluation Systems

A fourth point is that no matter how objective and quantitative the results of any job evaluation system may appear to be, they are in fact derived largely from subjective value judgments by the individuals or organization administering the evaluation process. A job evaluation system can provide an orderly framework for making such value judgments and a format for expressing their results in quantities that can be compared, combined, or manipulated in accordance with weighted formulas. But, at bottom, the process is still inherently judgmental and the results are merely expressions of a series of individual decisions about what the particular employer chooses to value, and to what degree.

As with most matters of business or managerial judgment, the values and choices that underlie job evaluations are rarely static. Instead, they are constantly changing to reflect altered conditions. Consequently, the evaluated "worth" of a particular job, even if expressed in numerical terms, is not a scientific measurement of some constant, quantifiable property inherent in the job itself. It is merely a composite of judgmental decisions reflecting the relationship of a particular job to a particular organization's current scale of values at a particular point in time.

Efforts to remove biases from these value judgments are laudable, of course. Indeed, many job evaluation systems include

---

[14]As one treatise has observed with respect to the Nixon administration's wage and price controls:

> When controls were finally ended in 1974 with inflation racing ahead at more than 10 percent annually, there was a general consensus that, though controls might have accomplished some specific goals for a limited time, over the long run they were both ineffective in regulating powerful market forces and disruptive of the economic system.

S. Levitan, G. Mangum, and R. Marshall, *Human Resources and Labor Markets* (1981), p. 423.

procedures designed to minimize the effects of race and sex-related stereotypes in the preparation of job descriptions, the selection and weighting of compensable factors, and other steps of the evaluation process. But to the extent that purely subjective value judgments are concerned, bias, like beauty, is apt to reside in the eye of the beholder. Office workers are likely to feel that the stresses of their jobs are undervalued in relation to the physical effort of factory work. Factory workers may feel just the opposite. And if most of the office workers in a given organization are women and most of the factory workers are men, each group may believe that the employer's job evaluation system is biased against their sex. An outside arbiter could be called in to review all job evaluations, but what assurance could there be that the arbiter's judgments would be any more bias-free than the immediate parties'?

Another alternative would be to democratize job evaluations by submitting all issues involving value judgments to a committee on which each race and sex group and each major job category in the workforce was represented. But again, there could be no guarantee that majoritarian value judgments by such a committee would be any less influenced by biases than individual value judgments by a business manager. This is not to say that it is not desirable or useful for employers to obtain input from affected groups in the workforce in evaluating jobs. To the extent practicable, measures that involve employees with diverse interests in a job evaluation study can help in some situations to promote a perception among employees that the results of the study are fair. But the fact that a particular determination of job worth is acceptable to the majority of a committee, or even to the entire committee, does not make it any more or less subjective, nor necessarily any more or less bias-free. Multiple biases do not necessarily cancel each other out, and an evaluation made by a committee with a number of members representing conflicting interests or points of view can hardly be said to be a bias-free judgment.

The Market Factor

A final point is that job evaluation as practiced in the United States is almost never a market-blind process as envisioned by

57

proponents of "pay equity" measures. On the contrary, practically all such systems incorporate some mechanism to enable the employing organization to maintain desired relationships between its pay scales and the external market rates for similar jobs.[15] Some make a direct connection, using the market as the primary determinant of wage rates for all jobs. Others survey the market rates for selected "bench mark" jobs and then extrapolate the rates for other positions by means of comparative evaluations of job content. Still other systems begin with an analysis of job content from a strictly internal standpoint, and then group jobs into pay grades or ranges for which pay rates are established by reference to external market data. Some of the more innovative systems undertake to determine the separate market values of various individual job elements or job-element "clusters" and incorporate them into the job evaluation process before any overall point total or ranking for each job has been established.

Job evaluation is one step toward establishing prices for jobs, but there usually has to be another step to relate internal job value assessments to external labor market rates. When that is done, there typically has to be a good deal of adjusting to reconcile between internal and external considerations before pay rates can be finalized. These ties to the market exist because without them, job evaluations would serve no practical purpose. The labor market still dictates at least the minimums that most employers have to pay to attract and retain workers with the needed skills, and the economic position of the firm relative to its competitors generally dictates the maximums it can pay. Without some mechanism for reconciling internal job value determinations with external market rates, few organizations could survive indefinitely. They would eventually either lose essential workers to higher paying firms or destroy their competitive position because of excessive labor costs.

Government agencies are typically much less directly sensitive to competitive market pressures than profit-oriented busi-

---

[15] As practiced, "job evaluation identifies and differently weights compensable factors to maximize the relationship between them and the wages for key jobs which are assumed to reject the market. Thus, the actual criterion of job evaluation is not worth in a job content sense, but market wages." G. Hildebrand, "The Market System," in *Comparable Worth: Issues and Alternatives*, ed., E. Livernash (1980), p. 63.

58

nesses, and, thus, are free to give more weight to internal equity considerations. But even civil service systems cannot afford generally to maintain pay scales that are substantially out of line with prevailing market rates if they wish to attract and retain qualified workers without exceeding budgetary limitations. Thus, the notion of a market-blind system of evaluation that will yield measurements of inherent job worth is ultimately illusory.[16]

Summary of Basic Characteristics

Recapping briefly, there are five basic characteristics of job evaluation that bear importantly on its potential for use as an instrument to effectuate a governmentally-imposed policy of equal pay for jobs of comparable worth:

1. Job evaluation systems exist in almost infinite varieties, and no one system is suitable for use in all circumstances;

2. Job evaluation systems generally are designed to serve multiple objectives for the employing organization, not just to achieve "internal equity;"

3. Job evaluation necessarily involves managerial decisions involving the economic condition of the employer that can properly be made only by the employing organization itself;

4. Job evaluation results are based largely on subjective and frequently changing value judgments by those conducting the evaluation process; and

5. In practice, job evaluation is not a market-free process, but necessarily includes mechanisms for reconciling internal wage relationships with external labor market factors.

Given these fundamental characteristics, it is fair to question whether job evaluation can provide an effective means of implementing a general legal mandate for comparable worth. Cer-

---

[16]As one federal appeals court concluded after reflecting on this subject in the context of a wage discrimination suit brought under Title VII of the Civil Rights Act of 1964:

Appellants' theory ignores economic realities. The value of the job to the employer represents but one factor affecting wages. Other factors may include the supply of workers willing to do the job and the ability of the workers to band together to bargain collectively for higher wages. We find nothing in the text and history of Title VII suggesting that Congress intended to abrogate the laws of supply and demand or other economic principles that determine wage rates for various kinds of work. We do not interpret Title VII as requiring an employer to ignore the market in setting wage rates for genuinely different work classifications.

Christensen v. State of Iowa, 563 F.2d 353, 356 (8th Cir. 1977).

tainly, voluntary job evaluation programs undertaken by employers unilaterally or with union participation can be helpful in developing pay relationships that employees will perceive as equitable. Certainly, the courts can police job evaluation systems under existing laws to ensure that they are not designed or administered with discriminatory intent. But is it realistic for the law to expect *more* than this from job evaluation?

Could the government, for example, impose a standardized system of job evaluation on all employers as a means of implementing comparable worth, without significantly intruding on basic, entirely legitimate business decisions which are considered to be management prerogatives? Could job evaluation standards imposed and/or monitored by outside regulators be expected to serve the varied internal managerial and administrative purposes for which job evaluation is practiced in the U.S. today? Would government-imposed or court-enforced job evaluation requirements create an obstacle to the attainment of external competitiveness and other essential organizational goals? Is it reasonable to expect that regulators or courts untrained in management and unfamiliar with all the particulars of a given industry or organization could achieve greater internal equity in pay rates than presently exists?

These questions must be seriously explored and realistic answers found before job evaluation can be considered as a fundamental part of proposals to require employers to provide equal pay for jobs of comparable worth.

Chapter Seven

POTENTIAL UNINTENDED CONSEQUENCES OF A COMPARABLE WORTH POLICY

The preceding chapters raise a series of questions about the valuation of jobs that must be answered satisfactorily before anyone can say with assurance that a policy of comparable worth would really work to promote pay equity. While these questions certainly need to be addressed in any responsible debate on this subject, they are not the only issues that remain to be examined and answered. Just as important as knowing whether such a policy would achieve its intended goal is knowing whether it would have any unintended side effects, either favorable or adverse. A growing number of scholarly studies have raised concerns about potential consequences of a broad-scale comparable worth policy.

The National Academy of Sciences Report

As part of the conclusion of its report on "equal pay for jobs of equal value," the National Academy of Sciences committee found that there was a need to give careful thought to the potential impact of such a policy on the economic viability of firms as well as on the employment opportunities for women and minorities.[1] The NAS report observed:

> [S]ince much of the wage differential arises because women work in low-wage firms and men work in high-wage firms, however,

---

[1] *Women, Work, and Wages*, p. 92.

61

even a comparable worth approach, applied to single firms, would not entirely eliminate the differential. For this reason and because, given the complexity of labor markets, a comparable worth strategy may have unanticipated and unintended effects, it cannot be viewed as a panacea.[2]

This final caution in the NAS discussion must not be taken lightly. Any policy that involves intervention in the labor market necessarily requires full consideration of the complexity of labor markets and all the forces that influence market outcomes. Because so many factors are influential, policies to alter outcomes that focus only on selected factors may not have the intended effects. Indeed, as the NAS report recognized, "because of the complexity of market processes, actions intended to have one result may well turn out to have other, even perverse, consequences."[3]

In this regard, it is important to recognize that a comparable worth policy would require more than just a one-time intervention into the labor market. Initial implementation of such a policy would presumably require the evaluation of every job and an upward wage adjustment in every predominantly-female or predominantly-minority job found to have been undervalued in the past. But the process would not stop there. Alterations in the wage relationships between such jobs would inevitably lead to changes in supply and demand within the affected job categories. Resultant shortages of supply in specific classifications could, in turn, necessitate additional increases in wages in order to attract workers with needed skills. But under a comparable worth policy, such increases would then force equivalent increases in other, equally-rated classifications. These increases could lead to further changes in supply and demand, and so on. Moreover, since the content of jobs seldom remains static for long, employers would have to be reevaluating jobs and adjusting wage rates continuously as products, workloads and operating methods changed, in order to maintain pay relationships that would always be defensible from the standpoint of comparable worth. Thus, in considering the likelihood of unintended consequences, it should be understood that any policy of comparable worth would almost

---

[2]*Ibid*, p. 67.
[3]*Women, Work, and Wages*, pp. 65-66.

62

certainly have to be an ongoing policy whose implementation would extend over many years.

Comments by Experts on Counterproductive Consequences

Although the potential for unintended consequences has generally been overlooked in the pay equity debate, the conclusions of several experts who have examined the possible impact of a policy designed simply to raise the wages of workers in predominantly-female jobs deserve attention. Professor Mark Killingsworth of Rutgers University found that a policy requiring wage increases for predominantly-female, low-paying jobs would provide immediate benefits for the women in such jobs. He believes, however, that other less desirable effects would then follow:

> Unfortunately, requiring wage increases for predominantly-female low-paying jobs is likely to have serious, albeit, unintended, adverse side-effects, not merely for women as a whole, but for older cohorts of women workers in particular.[4]

Professor Killingsworth demonstrates his conclusions by the use of a model economy in which Job A is a predominantly-female low-wage job and job B is a higher paying job held by both men and women:

> First, since the A wage rises, firms' demands for A workers will fall, leading to unemployment for some workers now in job A— who are disproportionately female. Second, the increase in the A wage raises labor costs and therefore prices; so consumers' demand falls. As consumers' demand falls, employer's output will contract, leading to decreases in the demand for job B (and, thus, to decreases in the demands for both male *and female* workers in job B. In turn, the decline in the demand for job B will lead to unemployment and/or lower wages for both men and women initially in job B.[5]

---

[4]M. Killingsworth, "The Case For and Economic Consequences of Comparable Worth: Analytical, Empirical and Policy Questions," a paper prepared for a Seminar on Comparable Worth Research sponsored by the Commission on Behavioral and Social Sciences and Education, National Academy of Sciences/National Research Council, Hilton Head, South Carolina, October 7-8, 1983, p. 20. See also testimony of Dr. Killingsworth at U.S. Congress Joint Economic Committee Hearings on Women in the Workforce, April 10, 1984.
[5]*Ibid*, pp. 20-21.

He concludes that, in the short run, the idea that raising wages in low-paid, predominantly-female jobs "will help older cohorts of women who are locked into those jobs is at best half-true: such a policy will certainly benefit *some* of these women but, by reducing the total demand for such jobs, will necessarily harm the rest of them."[6]

Professor Killingsworth then assumes in his model that, over a longer period of time after adoption of the wage increase for job A, supplies of labor for job A and job B will adjust to the changed wages for the jobs.

> However, in the long run as in the short run, the policy of raising pay for job A will also have several adverse side-effects. First, as in the short-run case, firms' demands for workers for job A will fall as the A wage rises. This will reduce employment of workers in job A, leading to unemployment for some individuals who would otherwise be in job A. (Since women are overrepresented in job A, this unemployment will hit women harder than men.) Second, the increase in the A wage *relative to* the wage for both men and women in job B attracts workers towards job A and away from job B. This reduces employment of both men *and women* in job B. In the absence of any restraint on the A wage, this increase in the supply of labor to job A would drive the A wage back to its original level. However, the comparable worth policy prevents the A wage from falling; instead, the increased supply to job A turns into more unemployment. Finally, since total employment in job A declines and employment of both men and women in job B also declines, production drops. The drop in production results in an increase in the price level.[7]

Professor Killingsworth's model is in line with the conclusions drawn by several other economists who have examined the potential side-effects of a policy that simply provides wage increases for predominantly-female jobs. Professor George Hildebrand of Cornell University, analyzing the economic ramifications of a policy of comparable worth, concluded:

> We already know enough about the consequences of the policy to be able to predict that it will increase unemployment still further, having the greatest effect on low-productivity workers. In fact, because of the cumulative consequences of discrimi-

---

[6]*Ibid*, p. 21.
[7]*Ibid*, p. 22. (footnote omitted).

nation in the past, many of those who are displaced will be women who are black or from other minority groups whose earnings already place them at the poverty line or near to it.[8]

Professor Hildebrand observed that a comparable worth policy would be likely to increase unemployment in three specific ways:

First, as with the minimum wage it will raise the price of . . . workers without improving their productivity. In consequence, employers will be induced to lay part of the group off to hold down the enforced rise in their costs. Unlike the minimum wage, comparable worth would affect many more workers because it is intended to reach much further into the labor market. Second, for the low-paid women working in the numerous small or even tiny firms, the imposed rise in labor costs will bring about either much bankruptcy or voluntary closure. Disemployment of these workers will follow. Third, in larger firms the imposed increase in labor costs will create an incentive to substitute capital and to revise plant or shop organization to replace low-paid women or alternatively, to raise hiring standards so that fewer workers of either sex who are more productive can replace them.[9]

Another economic analysis, by Professor C. M. Lindsay, reached similar conclusions. He observes that implementing a policy of comparable worth will increase the wages of some women, but "considerable female unemployment will result, particularly in those occupations now predominantly filled by women, whose wages will be boosted to the level of higher paying 'comparable' jobs."[10] Professor Lindsay explains that if the existing differential in wage rates has occurred as a result of the "crowding" of women into certain occupations, then there are already "too many" women in those occupations and "too few" women in others. "Raising wage rates in crowded occupations will aggravate this condition," he suggests.[11]

---

[8]G. H. Hildebrand, "The Market System," in *Comparable Worth: Issues and Alternatives*, ed., E. Livernash (1980), p. 105.

[9]*Ibid*, p. 106.

[10]C. M. Lindsay, *Equal Pay for Comparable Work: An Economic Analysis of a New Antidiscrimination Doctrine*, published by Law and Economics Center, University of Miami (1980), p. 33. See also testimony of Dr. Lindsay at the U.S. Congress Joint Economic Committee Hearings on Women in the Workforce, April 10, 1984.

[11]*Ibid*, p. 33. Professor Lindsay adds that if, on the other hand, the existing "differential between jobs reflects market clearing conditions, considerable economic distortion will be introduced by compelling employers to equalize wage rates."

Furthermore, Lindsay points out, arbitrarily raising wages in particular occupations can trigger other fundamentally counterproductive effects. "Wage increases in occupations now filled by women will raise the cost of labor above its marginal revenue product." Thus, Lindsay suggests, "Employers will then use less of this now-more-costly resource, and some women will lose their jobs. This employment effect, though not yet empirically examined, could conceivably be quite large."[12] While declining to estimate the exact extent of the resulting unemployment among women now in predominantly-female jobs, Professor Lindsay does suggest that the impact of comparable worth on these women could be similar to the impact of the minimum wage law on the employment of teenagers.[13]

Cautions Offered By Other Experts

Cautions about potential negative consequences accompanying the implementation of a comparable worth policy also have come from Dr. Daniel Glasner, of the Hay consulting organization, in his testimony at a Congressional hearing on equal pay for work of comparable value:

> Legislating increases of women's average pay to equal men's average pay would upgrade the economic condition of women, but the inflationary and unemployment consequences could be considerable. How can you use legislation and regulations to accelerate progress toward pay equity without those disruptions of the general economy which will inherently counteract any progress that is envisioned?[14]

In prior hearings, other witnesses offered similar observations.[15]

---

[12]*Ibid.*

[13]Professor Lindsay cites a study by Finis Welch, *Minimum Wages: Issues and Evidence* (Washington, D.C., AEI, 1978), which concluded that, depending on age, the minimum wage reduces employment among teenagers from fifteen to 46 percent. Lindsay observes, "The large wage increases implicit under the 'equal pay for comparable work' doctrine could certainty have a similar effect on employment in the affected occupations."

[14]See Testimony at Joint Hearings on Pay Equity before the Subcommittees on Human Resources, Civil Service, and Compensation and Employee Benefits, of the Committee on Post Office and Civil Service, House of Representatives, 97th Cong., 2d Sess., September 21, 1982.

[15]See, e.g., testimony of Richard Whalen, President of the National Public Employers Labor Relations Association, during hearings on wage discrimination before the Equal Employment Opportunity Commission, April 28-30, 1980, pp. 477-496 ("the comparable worth theory will harm most the groups that it seeks to assist by forcing disproportionate layoffs of minorities and females").

Professor Herbert Northrup of the University of Pennsylvania, an expert in labor management relations, has suggested that a government-imposed system of comparable worth not grounded in market realities would destabilize the internal wage relationships within a company which are used as a means of establishing an orderly wage structure and of facilitating and encouraging an orderly job progression.

> In short, the bargaining process breaks down without stable wage relationships. Negotiators for new contracts find themselves unable to deal adequately with the major issue, because their time and energies are consumed by attempting to settle a myriad of almost individual disputes concerning whether employees are compensated fairly in relation to others. Moreover, the settlement of one issue is as likely to trigger additional disputes as it is to bring peace. Job relationship disputes involve not only compensation but social and peer prestige as well. If the multiple spindle grinder operator was being paid the same wage rate as the shaper operator, and then the latter's rate is raised, the former is likely to become quite upset. He is now lower rated in money and, from his perspective, perhaps in social standing as well. Without criteria upon which to rely, the union is forced to process a huge volume of grievances, and the company is faced with potential labor disputes, or a constantly rising wage bill, or both. The results can be chaos, declining market share, lost jobs, or even business failure. The larger the facility, of course, the more difficult and expensive are the problems that arise.[16]

Potential Effect on International Competition

The economic analyses discussed above focus primarily on the potential consequences of comparable worth for the domestic U.S. economy. A related subject that needs additional serious study is how a policy that mandates increases in wage rates without increasing productivity would affect the competitive position of U.S. firms in international markets. Recent experience in steel, automobile manufacturing and other industries once dominated by U.S. firms has made employers and economists painfully aware that, in today's global economy, when the wage component of production costs of American products rises too

---

[16]H.R. Northrup, "Wage Setting and Collective Bargaining," in *Comparable Worth: Issues and Alternatives*, ed., E. Livernash (1980), pp. 122-23.

high in comparison with that of foreign-made goods, U.S. workers lose jobs to overseas competitors and the overall U.S. economy suffers.[17]

Foreign Experience Inconclusive

In attempting to forecast the consequences of a new economic or social policy, it is sometimes useful to look to the experience of foreign countries that have previously adopted the same type of policy. Such comparisons can be enlightening, provided they take sufficient account of differences between the systems of the countries being compared, as well as differences in surrounding circumstances that might prevent the experience of one country from being repeated in the other. To date, however, foreign experience with policies requiring equal pay for work of "equal value" or "comparable worth" has generally been too limited and inconclusive to shed much light on the probable consequences of implementing such a concept in the United States.[18]

The experience of Australia, however, deserves special attention because it has often been cited in the current debate as evidence that a comparable worth policy can be implemented without disruptive consequences. Thus, Robert E. Gregory of Australian National University suggested, in a statement delivered in 1980, that the government of Australia had successfully raised women's wages during the mid-1970's without disrupting female employment.[19] Mr. Gregory's conclusions are challenged, however, in the recent analysis by Professor Killingsworth cited above. Killingsworth points out that a study by Gregory and Duncan published in 1981 showed that increases in women's wages attributable to the new pay policy led to reduc-

[17]*Ibid*, p. 133. Increases in hourly compensation that exceed gains in labor productivity result in increased unit labor costs for manufacturers. As a recent study observed, because "labor costs are a principal component of the costs of manufactured goods, unit labor costs play a major role in conjunction with the exchange rates among currencies in determining the relative prices of goods offered for sale on the world market." D. Alvarez and B. Cooper, "Productivity Trends in Manufacturing in the U.S. and 11 Other Countries," *Monthly Labor Review*, Jan. 1984, pp. 54-55.

[18]For a detailed discussion of foreign experiences with policies embracing these concepts, see J. Bellace, "A Foreign Perspective," *Comparable Worth: Issues and Alternatives*, ed., E. Livernash (1980), pp. 137-172.

[19]See Testimony of R. E. Gregory, Hearings on Job Segregation and Wage Discrimination before Equal Employment Opportunity Commission, April 28-30, 1980, pp. 615-616.

68

to reductions in female employment.[20] "The most interesting aspect of Australia's experience," in Killingsworth's view, "is that the policy's side-effects appear to have been generally adverse," and that increases in women's wages attributable to the policy "led to reductions in female employment (below the level that would be expected solely on the basis of secular and business cycle factors), relative to men's employment" in manufacturing, in services and in all industries combined. Only in the public authority and community services sector did the policy have only a negligible effect on women's relative employment.[21] Thus, to the extent that the Australian experience can serve as a model for this country, it appears that Australia has not been immune to the counterproductive consequences discussed earlier in this chapter.

As with all attempts to use foreign experience as a model for legislation in this country, it is essential to examine the basic differences between the Australian and U.S. systems to determine the utility of any comparison. In Australia, for example, federal and state tribunals establish separate minimum wage levels for thousands of different jobs. These minimum levels are legally binding, but the parties are free to negotiate over-award wage levels through a modified procedure of collective bargaining. For many years, the sex of the worker was a basic component in this minimum wage calculation; the tribunals assumed that a male worker was maintaining a family and that a female worker was not. In 1969, the tribunals began to introduce the concept of equal pay for work of the same or like nature and of equal value. In 1972, this was broadened to allow gradual introduction of a principle of equal pay for work of equal value, so that sex might also be eliminated as a criterion in the minimum wage awards

---

[20] See M. Killingsworth, "The Case For and Economic Consequences of Comparable Worth: Analytical, Empirical and Policy Questions" (1983), *supra* note 4, pp. 23-24. Professor Killingsworth examines the findings of R. Gregory and R. Duncan reported in "Segmented Labor Market Theories and the Australian Experience of Equal Pay for Women," *Journal of Post Keynesian Economics* (1981), 3:403-428. See also the discussion of the Australian experience in Killingsworth's testimony at U.S. Congress Joint Economic Committee Hearings on Women in the Workforce, April 10, 1984.

[21] See Killingsworth, *ibid*, p. 23. Professor Killingsworth points out that the Gregory-Duncan study shows that Australia's policy *raised* the female *unemployment* rate. He observes that the econometric analysis by Gregory and Duncan shows that the policy had a statistically significant negative effect on the growth rate of women's employment, reducing it below the rate that otherwise would have occurred.

for predominantly-female jobs. Thus, by 1975, the sex of the worker was removed from all minimum wage determinations.

Mr. Gregory has explained that the result of these changes has been that the average earnings of a full-time female worker, relative to the average earnings of a full-time male worker, have increased from 58 percent to 77 percent.[22] Significantly, Mr. Gregory also has noted that the "equalization process" in Australia occurred during a period of significant growth and expansion in the economy of Australia.[23] The United States has never had a sex differential in its minimum wage laws and it remains questionable whether the "equalization process" in Australia closely resembles the comparable worth theory being advocated in this country. Thus, the experience of foreign countries fails to provide any reliable indication that instituting comparable worth in the United States would not have a counterproductive impact. Indeed, as one expert who has studied compensation practices in many countries has concluded,

> most countries whose equal pay statutes or regulations contain the formulation "equal pay for work of equal value" have not yet had sufficient experience with the implications and application of this guarantee to determine with any accuracy whether it represents a significantly more far-reaching guarantee than the American "equal pay for equal work."[24].

In sum, a number of experts' views have raised serious questions about the consequences that might be expected to accompany implementation of a comparable worth system, and the experience of foreign countries provides no assurance that these experts' concerns are overstated. At a minimum, the observations of these experts serve as a caution that the comparable worth

---

[22]According to the International Labor Organization's 1983 Year Book of Labor Statistics, the earnings differential between men's and women's earnings in Australia widened between 1977 and 1982, although the statistics for the overall period of 1973 through 1982 do show a narrowing of the gap. A recent ILO report analyzing the statistics on earnings differences includes a warning about using such statistics for international comparisons because statistical concepts, definitions, sources and study scope often vary from one country to another. The report observes that: "A more scientific approach to salary gaps between men and women should take into account numerous factors such as the distribution of women according to occupations, branches of industry, the length of service in the company, the duration of work and whether it is part-time or night work."

[23]Testimony of R. Gregory, Hearings on Job Segregation and Wage Discrimination before Equal Employment Opportunity Commission, April 28-30, 1980, pp. 612-613.

[24]J. Bellace, "A Foreign Perspective," Comparable Worth: Issues and Alternatives, ed., E. Livernash (1980), p. 169.

theory must be examined in more detail before it can be considered the most practical approach to narrowing the pay gap. These questions, as well as the potential negative consequences for employees in low-paying predominantly-female jobs, were also recognized in the NAS report itself. Noting that increased wages for women in these jobs could have some unintended side effects, the NAS study suggested that "a comparable worth strategy might reduce employment either because employers shift to alternative, less labor-intensive methods of production or (if the labor costs were paid and passed on) because consumers might switch to other, less expensive goods or services."[25]

The NAS report also pointed out the fundamental truth that "in our economy not everyone can have a 'good,' high-paying job. Our economy generates low-wage jobs as well as high-wage jobs; attempts to prevent their being filled in this country may simply result in the exportation of low-wage jobs."[26] Narrowing the pay gap will be meaningful only if it can be done in a way that does not jeopardize the continued availability of plentiful job opportunities for American workers. The possibility of serious counterproductive consequences deserves additional attention.

[25] *Women, Work, and Wages*, p. 67.
[26] *Ibid*, p. 66.

Chapter Eight

COSTS AND BENEFITS OF COMPARABLE WORTH VERSUS AN EQUAL OPPORTUNITY APPROACH

One of the most publicized aspects of the trial court's decision in the *State of Washington* case was the magnitude of the verdict. Initial estimates suggested that the state government would be required to pay out some 800 million to one billion dollars in back pay and wage increases.[1] The State's entire budget is approximately 10 billion dollars annually. The State had urged the court not to order immediate implementation of wage adjustments because of the tremendous costs involved. Rather, the State pointed out that earlier in 1983 it had adopted a program of phased-in wage adjustments that would fully implement the pay levels suggested by the State's job evaluation studies over a 10-year period. Attorneys for the State argued that the government could not afford a quicker remedy and urged the judge to let the 10-year, phased-in solution stand. Specifically, the State pointed to its current lack of revenue because of the depressed condition of the forest industry, which provides much of the State's tax revenues. It also emphasized that available state revenues were already committed to such programs as education, prisons, and social services, and that the State Constitution mandates a balanced budget.[2] The court rejected the State's plea.

---

[1]T. Lewin, "A New Push to Raise Women's Pay," *New York Times*, Jan. 1, 1984, Section 3, page 1; R. Walker, "Women's Push for 'Comparable Worth,'" *Christian Science Monitor*, Jan. 19, 1984.
[2]See *AFSCME v. State of Washington*, 578 F. Supp. at 868, 33 Fair Empl. Prac. Cas. at 823.

Thus, if the trial court's ruling is sustained on appeal, the State of Washington will be faced with the difficult, practical problem of how to come up with the money to fund its comparable worth system of compensation.

The Relevance of Cost Considerations

Similarly, before comparable worth is adopted as a mandatory policy for other employers, the questions of how much it will cost and where the funds will come from will have to be addressed. This is not to suggest that cost should be the sole, or even the primary consideration in deciding whether or not to adopt comparable worth. To the extent that some part of the pay gap results from compensation practices that discriminate against women and minority workers, those practices cannot be justified merely because they may happen to cost less than nondiscriminatory practices. But, as was stressed at the outset of this paper, the issue is not whether we should eliminate unfair and discriminatory compensation practices. Rather, the issue is whether comparable worth theory provides a practical, effective way of doing so. If it does *not*, then comparable worth should be rejected even if the costs involved would be minimal.

On the other hand, if, after thorough consideration of all the questions raised in the preceding chapters, it appears that a policy of comparable worth is needed and would work to effectuate the goal of pay equity, then the question of cost cannot be avoided. As the State of Washington's experience illustrates, any costs involved in implementing a comparable worth policy for state government employees are likely to affect the availability of funds for other important programs. It may be possible for a state government to raise taxes or adjust priorities to accommodate additional compensation costs for state employees, but sensible planning requires at a minimum that state policy-makers have some idea in advance what the total costs will be. Similarly, if a mandatory comparable worth requirement is to be imposed on the private sector, its total cost should be known in advance in order that employers, consumers and governments can anticipate its economic effects and plan accordingly. For if the total cost of implementing comparable worth on a nationwide basis is as great as some experts have estimated, failure to plan in advance for its impact would have serious economic consequences.

Estimates of the Cost of Comparable Worth

Attempts to estimate the potential costs of comparable worth are hampered at this time, of course, by the present lack of specific details about how the comparable worth theory might be put into practice. Inevitably, the cost of administering a system based on comparable worth would depend substantially on the extent to which that system required the government to oversee or supplant the wage-setting practices of private and public employers. It is fair to assume that decisions on the relative worth of different jobs necessarily will involve more administrative complexity than a straight-forward decision as to whether two jobs involve equal work, but how much more is unknown.[3]

In addition to the very substantial costs of administration, there also would be costs represented by increased wage rates. (It is assumed here that any comparable worth system would follow the policy of the Equal Pay Act and require that wage rates be equalized by raising the lower wage rates to the level of the highest rate paid for "comparable" work, rather than by decreasing the higher wage rates. None of the proponents has suggested that equilibrium be achieved by even partial use of the latter method.) There have been several estimates of the total dollars represented by such wage increases, but this, too, is a subject that needs considerable additional attention.

One estimate of the cost of comparable worth is particularly interesting because it is based directly on the gross pay gap statistics frequently cited by comparable worth proponents. This estimate comes from calculations by Dr. Daniel Glasner of the

---

[3]Depending upon what sort of mechanism might be established to implement a comparable worth policy, potential administrative costs could include the time of managers and consultants (and possibly employee representatives) spent in initially evaluating all jobs, reevaluating jobs each time a change in duties occurred or each time a labor market variation forced a wage adjustment, and explaining and defending job evaluations whenever an employee challenged their conclusions. Such tasks, and the accompanying expenses, are likely to be substantial, particularly when viewed in light of the unlimited variations of jobs that exist in the U.S. economy. For example, the 1980 Standard Occupational Classification lists 503 occupational categories. Specific job duties of persons within these classifications vary from one employer to another and from one work establishment to another. Because working conditions and labor markets can vary from one place of employment to another, the evaluation of jobs at one facility may not be applicable to similar jobs at another facility.

Hay Management Consultants, who describes himself as an advocate of "managed change." Accepting the comparable worth advocates' claims that women earn only about 60 cents for every dollar that men earn, Dr. Glasner calculates that to eliminate 80 percent of the pay gap would cost a total of 320 billion dollars in increased pay and benefits for women.[4] This one-year cost represents an increase in pay and benefits with no addition to the workforce and no increase in goods and services, and would add approximately 9.7 percent to the existing inflation rate.[5]

Because Dr. Glasner's cost calculations were developed using gross statistics, it appears to be an appropriate response to the often-quoted pay gap calculations, which also use gross statistics. As noted in earlier chapters, however, none of the statistical studies conducted thus far has been able to quantify and account for all of the generally accepted, nondiscriminatory factors that also contribute to the differential in male/female earnings, and therefore the premise that 80 percent of the pay gap is due to discrimination should not be accepted without more careful analysis.

Is There a Less Costly Alternative?

Gross statistical calculations do not accurately portray the "problem" or the "solution," and our equal employment policies are not designed to provide gross statistical remedies. Rather, our current equal opportunity laws are designed to apply to individual employers by prohibiting specific discriminatory employment practices. Similarly, our policies to eliminate sex-bias in compensation are not aimed at trying to assure that the average man and the average woman have the same income, regardless of differences in their work and lifestyle. Rather, they are aimed at remedying the specific causes of discrimination and at assuring equal treatment of women in all employment practices.

Unlike a theory of comparable worth which would impose notions of pay parity onto the workplace, our present policies emphasizing equal access and equal opportunity are aimed directly at those specific practices which have prevented women

---

[4]D. M. Glasner "Pay Equity Viewed From An Economic Perspective," AAA/LMRS Conference on Comparable Worth, Washington, D.C., January 23, 1984.
[5]*Ibid.*

and minorities from entering higher-paying jobs filled predominantly by white males. This equal opportunity approach need not be expensive to be effective. It requires that all jobs be made available to all interested, qualified applicants and that, once in those jobs, all workers be paid on the same basis, without regard to sex or race. This approach also requires that women and minorities have equal access to the training programs and career ladders that would lead them to the traditionally higher-paying jobs. Furthermore, this approach makes it illegal for employers to take into account the race or sex of workers when setting wages, and thus it also prohibits employers from manipulating job evaluation standards to the disadvantage of any protected group.

Thus, an effective equal opportunity approach promotes a very real form of pay equity without disrupting our economy or fundamentally altering our free market system. It facilitates a narrowing of the pay gap as sexual stereotypes change and more women move into non-traditional and higher-paying jobs, without penalizing employers for the market effects of occupational crowding that has taken place because of workers' individual preferences and societal factors outside the employment relationship.

Today, because of the changing nature of our economy, with the decline of so-called smokestack industries and the development of new technologies and industries, our society is in a particularly good position to provide practical opportunities to women who desire new career alternatives. Affirmative action efforts to bring women into the higher-paying jobs in these newer industries will not be impeded by the numerous hurdles that faced those who sought to increase the number of females in high-paying jobs in mines, steel mills and other older industries.[6]

The policy of equal opportunity has already had a noticeable impact on the occupations held by women in the labor force. In

---

[6]Recent occupational projections by the Bureau of Labor Statistics indicate that, between now and 1995, "rapid expansion of high technology will spur the growth of scientists, engineers, technicians, and computer specialists. They will be required to design, develop, and use high technology products such as computers, scientific and medical instruments, communication equipment, and robots. Employment in these occupations has generally grown faster than the economy as a whole and most are expected to continue to do so." G. Silvestri, J. Lukasiewicz, and M. Einstein, "Occupational Employment Projections Through 1995," *Monthly Labor Review*, U.S. Department of Labor, Nov. 1983, p. 37.

the past twenty years, many women have moved into tradition-ally-male jobs. While a substantial number of women (55%) began the 1980's in traditionally-female clerical and service oc-cupations, significant numbers of women had moved into profes-sional-technical jobs with higher earnings. As the table below shows,[7] for example, of the total number of people employed as accountants in 1960, only 16.4 percent were women. By 1980, that percentage had risen to 38.1. Similar increases are evident in other occupations. Between 1970 and 1980, significant num-bers of women moved into the executive, managerial and ad-ministrative positions traditionally held by men.[8]

In its final report, the National Academy of Sciences stated that policies "designed to promote equal access to all employ-

---

[7]This table shows the number of women in particular occupations as a percentage of all workers in that occupation in 1960 and 1980. The statistics are from the U.S. Bureau of Labor Statistics and the Bureau of the Census.

	Females as a percent of Total employed in occupation	
Occupation	1960	1980
Accountants and Auditors	16.4	38.1
Assemblers	43.7	49.5
Bakers	15.9	40.7
Bank Officials/Financial Managers	12.2	33.6
Bus Drivers	9.8	45.8
Buyers/Purchasing Agents	17.7	33.6
Carpenters	0.4	1.6
Engineers	0.9	4.6
Lawyers/Judges	3.3	14.0
Mechanics, including automotive	1.1	3.4
Physicians/Osteopaths	6.8	13.4
Protective Services (Police, Guards, Firefighters)	4.1	11.8
Printing craft workers	11.0	22.7
Restaurant, Cafeteria and Bar Mgrs.	24.0	39.4
Sales Mgrs./Dept. Heads (Retail)	28.2	40.5
Tailors	20.0	46.2
Teachers (College and Univ.)	21.3	36.6
Teachers (except College and Univ.)	71.6	70.8
Writers, Artists and Entertainers	34.2	42.1

See "Detailed Occupation of the Experienced Civilian Labor Force by Sex for the United States and Regions: 1980 and 1970," Supplementary Report issued March 1984 by the U.S. Bureau of the Census.

[8]A recent study comparing 1970 and 1980 occupational data concluded that in terms of actual changes of employment during the 1970's, the most significant change in the distribution of the sexes was that there were many more females in the "executive, administrative, and managerial" group. The study noted that while "in 1970, only 18 percent of managers were women, a rise in the percentage twice that for the overall labor force occurred during the decade." In 1980, the managerial group was 30.5 percent women. N. Rytina and S. Bianchi, "Occupational Reclassification and Changes in Distribution by Gender," *Monthly Labor Review*, March 1984, pp. 14-16.

78

ment opportunities will affect the under payment of women workers only slowly."[9] At least in part this criticism reflects the fact that our laws guaranteeing equal employment opportunity can act directly to eliminate only those portions of the differential that may be the result of discrimination by employers. It should not be assumed, however, that a comparable worth approach would be implemented and made effective overnight. In Washington State, for example, the potential cost of funding a comparable worth system was a significant factor in causing the state to delay action on the results of its comparable worth study, begun in 1974. In 1983, when the state did pass comparable worth legislation, potential costs were again a factor in the state's decision to use a ten-year implementation period.

In summary, cost must not be a primary consideration in our commitment to end employment discrimination. The questions about the comparable worth theory raised throughout this paper must be addressed and answered, even if comparable worth carries no cost to society or employers. But the Washington State experience makes it clear that at some point there must be consideration of the very practical question of where the revenue will come from to fund a comparable worth compensation system. Clearly, this is an issue which needs additional study. Whatever the total cost of comparable worth, however, it appears that there is an alternative approach to narrowing the pay gap which would not involve the potential negative economic consequences and costs associated with comparable worth. That is, an effectively-administered approach emphasizing equal access to higher-paying jobs for women and minorities. This approach need not be expensive, and it attacks directly whatever portion of the pay differentials between males and females and between whites and minorities may be the result of employment discrimination.

---

[9]*Women, Work, and Wages*, pp. 66-67.

Chapter Nine

CONCLUSION

The debate over "pay equity" has received widespread national attention following the trial court's decision in the Washington State case.[1] As discussed earlier, Washington State had conducted a series of studies of its compensation practices and decided that it would shift to a new compensation system—based on a comparable worth study—which assigned higher values to many predominantly-female job classifications among the State employees. The State's plan was to implement the comparable worth system over a ten-year period, from 1983 to 1993. The court, however, found that such phased-in implementation was inadequate. In the court's view, the State's failure to begin immediately paying employees their evaluated worth, according to the provisions of the State's comparable worth study, was illegal discrimination. Declaring that "Title VII remedies are *now*," the court ordered that the State implement at once the wage rates indicated in the study and reimburse employees in predominantly-female jobs for wages lost by reason of the State's failure to act sooner.

The irony of this particular defendant finding itself subject to a multi-million dollar verdict for employment discrimination did not pass without comment. The judge observed:

> The Defendant argues that it is ironic that the State of Washington was the first in the nation to consider and adopt the comparable worth rating system, and now is the first to be penalized with a

---

[1]*AFSCME v. State of Washington*, 578 F. Supp. 846, 33 Fair Empl. Prac. Cas. (BNA) 808 (W.D. Wash. 1983).

81

devastating court ruling. This court is of the opinion that it is indeed ironic and tragic that the State of Washington is in the eighth decade of the Twentieth Century attempting to use the American legal system to sanction, uphold and perpetuate sex bias. Defendants are struggling to maintain attitudes and concepts that are no longer acceptable under the provisions of Title VII.[2]

The judge's reasoning is now subject to review by a federal appeals court which must decide whether he gave adequate consideration to the state's entire compensation system and whether he properly interpreted and applied Title VII. These and other issues are vigorously disputed by the immediate parties to the case, as well as others who are familiar with the issues. Regardless of one's views of the court's reasoning or of the complicated fact situation that led up to the ruling in the Washington State case the judge's comment above reflects a tension that often has made it difficult to find any middle ground in the comparable worth debate.

The momentous increase in the number of women in the workplace, accompanied by the basic changes taking place in our society and its values, has led to honest questions about the fairness of certain compensation practices which were viewed in the past as being entirely equitable and fully in accord with the law. Comparable worth has been suggested as the answer to this dilemma and indeed, its theoretical simplicity has an emotional appeal. But that alone cannot guarantee that comparable worth in practice would be an effective tool.

To assess the feasibility of the comparable worth approach, it is necessary to recognize that what is at issue is a policy to be used in determining the relative worth of every job classification in thousands and thousands of workplaces on a day-to-day basis. Thus, an understanding of precisely how the theory would work is essential. In an effort to promote discussion and understanding, this paper has suggested numerous questions which must be addressed before comparable worth can be considered as a realistic approach to narrowing the pay gap.

With respect to the pay gap itself, it is necessary to examine what factors contribute to the differential in earnings between men and women. Similarly, the pay differential between whites

---

[2]33 Fair Empl. Prac. Cas. Cases at 824 n.17.

and minorities should be scrutinized. To what extent are these differences the result of practices by employers, as opposed to other factors? It is that portion of the gap, and that portion only, that equal employment opportunity policies can realistically be expected to close. Proposed solutions that ignore the numerous other causes of earnings differentials, such as historic educational inequities and social and cultural patterns that have led to uneven distributions of men and women in today's workforce, and merely assume that all of the underlying causes of the pay gap can be remedied through mandatory wage adjustments, are not likely to succeed.

The challenge, then, is to develop a comprehensive policy that recognizes the various causes of the pay gap and responds effectively to each cause through the most appropriate mechanism. As emphasized throughout this paper, if a comparable worth policy is to be a part of that approach, the threshold question is how will the comparable worth of different jobs be determined? Specifically, who will make that determination? Will it be a government agency, or a court, or will the worth be determined by the employer using standards issued by the government? If the latter, what will those standards be, and how will they be enforced? Are there any bias-free standards which allow the determination of the "intrinsic worth" of a job?

It has been suggested that job evaluation systems may be the means for making such determinations, but, as the preceding chapters have shown, job evaluation is not an objective or scientific methodology. Moreover, job evaluation systems are intended to operate in a dynamic fashion, to accommodate changes in job relationships. Job evaluation systems in this country generally are not designed to function totally without respect to the influences of the labor market. Will this market factor be recognized in a comparable worth system, and if so, how? And, once the worth of a job is determined, how will adjustments in that worth be made to accommodate changes in the market, changes in the economy, or changes in the employer's business?

Without an objective means of measuring job worth, the practicality of the comparable worth theory remains seriously flawed. The National Academy of Sciences recognized that such a system of measurement is needed before comparable worth can be considered a viable strategy for narrowing the earnings gap.

Beyond these fundamental problems, there remains the potential, also recognized by the NAS Report, that a theory of comparable worth which involves intervention in the labor market will carry unforeseen negative economic consequences. These potential side effects of comparable worth must receive more serious study before the concept can be considered a realistic alternative.

When assessed objectively and realistically, the manner in which our society might approach the challenge of narrowing the earnings gap is not limited to comparable worth. By breaking down the real and imagined barriers to traditionally-male jobs and by assuring that working women have equal access to the training programs and career ladders that lead to the higher-paying managerial, professional, and technical jobs in our society, we can continue the progress demonstrated over the past decade in the number of women moving into higher-paying and predominantly-male jobs. The laws and the machinery for such equal employment opportunity programs are already in place and enjoy strong support in the employer community. Women moving into these so-called traditionally-male jobs are guaranteed that they will receive equal pay for equal work. The net effect will be a narrowing of the earnings differential and a lessening of the present crowding of women workers into a few predominantly-female jobs. This, in turn, should lead to an increase in the rates of pay that women who remain in traditionally-female jobs can command for their labor in the market place. When the costs and benefits of the options are compared, a strong and effective policy of equal employment opportunity appears to be a viable and productive alternative to comparable worth as an approach to narrowing the differential.

84